GET DEBT FREE WITH ME

Kevin Heupel

For Ali – my one true love

Published in Denver, Colorado by Heupel Law. Printed in the United States of America.

Title ID: 4397391
ISBN-13: 978-0615866901
ISBN-10: 0615866905

This publication is designed to provide accurate and authoritative information with regard to the subject matter covered. It is sold with the understanding the publisher is not engaged in rendering legal, accounting, or other professional advice. If legal advice or other expert assistance is required, the services of a competent professional should be sought.

Acknowledgments

I'd like to acknowledge my past and current clients who had the courage to contact me during their darkest times and believed in my services to get them out of debt.

Foreword

Get Debt Free With Me

With the recent recession being called the worst economic crisis of our time, some people are struggling with overwhelming debt. Foreclosure rates are high, credit card payments are late, people are struggling to pay their bills and wonder if they can ever get out of debt.

Unfortunately, some people experience "paralysis through analysis" where they feel so overwhelmed by debt that they believe they are powerless to resolve their financial problems. They metaphorically stick their heads in the sand and hope the problem will disappear, either by winning the lottery or getting an inheritance. Some become so despondent that they even think about robbing a bank or believe that death is the only answer.

The good news is that there is a solution to every debt problem.

The key to resolving a debt problem is taking control of the situation. This is not easy to do without overcoming the six mental obstacles that keep a person stuck on the financial roller coaster of debt. The first part of this book will discuss the dysfunctional attitudes about debt and how to overcome them. The second part will provide an in-depth review of different type of options that are available for someone to get out of debt.

One matter that concerns people struggling with debt is what will happen to their credit score. That is a valid concern. Some solutions will lower your credit score and remain on your credit report for up to seven years. The good news is that you can begin rebuilding your credit as soon as you address the underlying debt problem. It often takes as little as 1-2 years to restore your credit if you follow the steps I describe in this book. The most important thing; however, is to deal with the debt first.

Many debt solutions are advertised (credit counseling, debt settlement, bankruptcy) and selecting the right one is difficult. There are misconceptions about how certain debt relief options work, which causes confusion and can feel so overwhelming that it is impossible to know what to do.

Getting over the emotional baggage that is keeping you trapped in inaction and seeking out solutions is the best way to rebuild your financial life. This book is the first step to overcoming the emotional impact of debt and getting out of debt.

If you want to immediately talk about your debt issues, then please call my office at (720) 443-4030. We offer free consultations to anyone who needs help.

Table of Contents

INTRODUCTION

For the past six years, I have helped almost 5,000 people get out of debt. Helping people get out of debt is now my life's work.

Prior to starting my own law firm, I was a Section Director of the Division of Professions and Occupations in Colorado's Department of Regulatory Agencies (DORA), a consumer protection agency. My section regulated licensed professionals in more than fifty professions (such as accountants, physicians, nurses, dentists, etc.[1]). DORA's mission was to ensure public protection by verifying the competency of applicants and pursuing disciplinary actions against violators.

When I left DORA to start my own law practice, I continued practicing administrative law. Instead of being a prosecutor, I was now defending the licensed professionals who received complaints issued by DORA. It was a difficult change and I did not enjoy the work. The government had all the power and my clients were at the mercy of DORA.

In 2007, I had the opportunity to learn bankruptcy law. I was immediately drawn to bankruptcy because it drew upon my prior experience as a corporate accountant. Also, unlike administrative law, debtors actually have most of the power in bankruptcy.

---

[1] http://cdn.colorado.gov/cs/Satellite?c=Page&childpagename=DORA%2FDORALayout&cid=1251627010865&p=1251627010865&pagename=CBONWrapper

What I enjoyed most about bankruptcy was the foreseeable nature of it. Bankruptcy is a surprisingly predictable practice. I can evaluate a case and predict with almost 99% certainty how bankruptcy will get a person out of debt and rebuild his financial life. As a result, I am able to offer my clients a "Money Back Guarantee," a practice unheard of in the legal field. In the six years that I have been practicing Bankruptcy Law, I have yet to refund any money.

My timing to become a bankruptcy attorney was excellent. I began practicing bankruptcy law before the financial crisis of 2008, which resulted in a storm of foreclosures throughout the country. Within two years of opening my practice, I went from being a sole practitioner to one of the largest bankruptcy firms in Colorado.

It was during this growth spurt I found my firm's mission: "We help good people like you get out of debt". What I discovered is that financial problems can happen to anyone. Some people think bankruptcy is the result of spending too much money. I discovered that bankruptcy is the result of something happening beyond a person's control; such as losing a job, loss of income, failed business, medical issues; etc. No one is immune from having debt problems and most of us are two paychecks away from having to file bankruptcy.

Choosing a bankruptcy attorney should be like choosing a surgeon. Would you rather trust your heart to a surgeon who has performed only a few open-heart procedures or one who has performed thousands with successful outcomes? The same principle applies to lawyers. Lawyers specialize in certain areas of law. It is important to select an attorney who has helped a lot of clients get out of debt. Experience translates into expertise, which can only be achieved by working on a high volume of cases.

Filing a lot of cases is only one aspect of being an effective bankruptcy attorney. It is also necessary to stay abreast of current case law. I belong to several organizations, such as the National Association of Consumer Bankruptcy Attorneys, American Bankruptcy Institute, and American College of Bankruptcy Consumers. I have been certified by the American Board of Certification as a bankruptcy specialist, which further differentiates me from other bankruptcy attorneys.

Not everyone is a candidate to file bankruptcy. Sometimes there are other debt relief options that provide better solutions. As such, I learned about credit counseling, debt settlement, offers in compromise, loan modifications, credit repair, and student loans in order to provide my clients with a full spectrum of options. Unfortunately, some attorneys try to force all of their clients into filing bankruptcy because it's the only area of law they understand. However, bankruptcy may not be the best solution for a particular client. I learned about all the options for getting out of debt so I could provide the best solution to my clients' unique situations.

Beyond having expertise, I understand what it's like to be consumed by debt (financially and emotionally). When I was growing up in the early 1980s, my father owned a used car lot and dreamt of owning a dealership. We were upper middle-class and lived a comfortable life in Colorado Springs. My father's dream finally came true when he had the opportunity to buy into a partnership for a Chrysler/Plymouth/ Honda/Volkswagen dealership in Scottsbluff, Nebraska. The family packed up and moved to the panhandle of Nebraska.

In this case, the timing could not have been worse. The country was in the midst of a recession, and farmers, who were the primary economic force in Scottsbluff, were hardest hit. Remember the Farm Aid concerts organized by Willie Nelson? Those concerts were to save family farms as so many farmers were going into foreclosure.

With farmers suffering, cars were not selling. Worse yet, my father's partner had not accurately disclosed the business' debts. The dealership had been failing and my father's investment simply bought time before the inevitable end. My father ultimately walked away from the business with nearly $100,000 of tax debt because his partner had not made payroll tax payments for several years. His partner didn't have to pay the taxes because he was drawing social security and would never have the financial means to repay it. Basically, the partner was "judgment proof" so the sole burden fell upon my father.

We returned to Colorado, but our lifestyle had changed dramatically. I had to get a job sooner than most kids my age in order to help support the family, buy my own car, and pay for college. The entire family had to start over.

Starting over is not easy. It hurts your psyche. I remember being angry that we were no longer "rich"; however, that experience taught me bad things can happen to good people. As a result, I know better than most people what my clients are going through because I've been through it myself.

I can help you get out debt by finding the best solution for you. I understand it is overwhelming when trying to get out of debt. There are a variety of options, which I explain in detail in this book, as well as the pros and cons of pursuing each approach. Not only do I want my clients to get out of debt, but I want them to be educated about the best solution and why it is going to work. When you understand the solution, it takes the fear away and brings financial security.

My first book was called, "Getting off the Roller Coaster of Debt" because the experience of being in debt is emotionally taxing. I've experienced it and have discovered that most people face six emotional hurdles when trying to get out of debt. I will discuss those challenges as well as the popular debt relief solutions.

> *"Thank you, Kevin Heupel, for making a difficult issue easier for us."*
>
> *-George & Joanne F.*

The right solution depends upon your unique situation and this book will give you an idea of where to start. If you want to immediately talk about your debt issues, then please call my office at (720) 443-4030. Remember, my mission is to help good people like you get out of debt.

CHAPTER ONE: The Six Emotional Hurdles to Overcoming Debt

Most people get into debt because of circumstances beyond their control. They lose a job, their income drops, or they have a medical or financial emergency at a time, they don't have 3-6 months of savings to carry them through the crisis. Without a sufficient reserve, it is common to use credit cards in what is expected to be a short-term problem. People pay for groceries, gas, utilities, and other basic needs with their credit cards while they look for a new job, rebuild their businesses, recover from an illness, or overcome whatever event caused them to need to rely on credit.

Using credit can create a false sense of security. When you "live" off credit, you don't realize how quickly the debt accumulates. If you lost a job that paid $4,000 per month and used credit cards for six months before you found another position, you would have accumulated approximately $24,000 of debt – plus interest! It shocks people how quickly the debt can accumulate when using credit with good intentions. This is, at least partially, because it doesn't feel like you're getting anything out of the debt you incurred. For example, in this scenario, your $24,000 hasn't bought you a new car that's sitting in your driveway; it has only allowed you to make ends meet.

Despite making the minimum monthly payments on your credit cards, your debt either remains the same or increases. You need to understand that credit card companies aren't in the business of lending money. They want cardholders to accumulate debt because they earn money on the high interest rates applied to the unpaid balances. That's why the bills always suggest a "minimum" payment so the credit card company ensures they can keep applying interest to a higher and higher balance. It's frustrating to make your monthly payments and realize that it's not reducing the debt. After a few months or years in this cycle, it's common to panic.

When panic sets in, decision making is impaired. People will dip into their retirement accounts to pay off some, but not all of the debt. Others will sell personal items to make a credit card payment because they feel they have no alternative.

Once the assets are sold and gone, people become distraught and start "robbing Peter to pay Paul." People will transfer debt balances from one credit card to another, ask a parent or friend to cosign a loan, or take out a second mortgage to pay off credit card debt. At this distressed stage a person is merely exchanging one bad debt for another.

This cycle can continue for a few months or up to several years before the person realizes he has too much debt to repay. At this point, he feels like a failure.

Most people use debt with the honorable intention of repaying their creditors. Ninety-nine percent of my clients want to repay their debts; however, the pain associated with financial failure is so strong that most people feel hopeless. They stop making minimum payments, and then have to endure nasty collection calls from ruthless creditors who reinforce these feelings of failure.

> *"Kevin Heupel has been fantastic thru this embarrassing experience for me. I am now able to start over in this new chapter of my life!"*
>
> *-Kathy C.*

Resolving debt problems can be easy; however, finding the emotional courage to identify the right solution can be challenging.

The following are six emotional hurdles that need to be to overcome in order to get out of debt.

Emotional Hurdle #1: TRUST

TRUST: "Assured reliance on the character, ability, strength or truth of someone or something; to place confidence." (Merriam-Webster's Collegiate Dictionary, Eleventh Edition)

A bank will give you an overdraft account, a line of credit, a car loan and multiple credit cards based upon your "credit score" – a numerical assessment of your creditworthiness[2]. However, once you are late on a payment, the bank will lower your credit limit, raise the interest rate, and file negative reports that affect your credit history, which makes it even more difficult to repay your debts. When you need help; however, don't trust the bank to assist you.

The Little Girl and Her Father[3]

A little girl and her father were crossing a bridge.

The father was kind of scared so he asked his little daughter, "Sweetheart, please hold my hand so that you don't fall into the river."

The little girl said, "No, Dad. You hold my hand."

"What's the difference?'" asked the puzzled father.

"'There's a big difference," replied the little girl.

"If I hold your hand and something happens to me, chances are that I may let your hand go. But if you

---

[2] http://en.wikipedia.org/wiki/Credit_score
[3] Variously attributed

hold my hand, I know for sure that no matter what
happens, you will never let my hand go."

In any relationship, the essence of trust is not in its bind,
but its bond. From the story above, we learn to rely on
someone and to expect them to hold our hand rather than
relying on ourselves. Sadly, the opposite is true when
dealing with financial matters. If you "hold hands" with
creditors, don't expect them to save you when you are
struggling with debt.

Peter Farquharson, executive director at Habitat for
Humanity, said: "Relationships of trust depend on our
willingness to look not only to our own interests, but also
the interests of others." When someone is in debt, he
looks to the banks, credit card companies, and collection
agencies for help. However, creditors look out for
themselves. A creditor does not care about your life
situation; he wants to get paid, and get paid immediately.

Trust is a very important factor for all relationships. When
trust is broken, it is the end of the relationship. Lack of
trust leads to suspicion, suspicion generates anger, anger
causes enmity, and enmity may result in pulling away.

The lack of willingness by creditors to work with people
makes it harder for someone struggling with debt to trust
any of the possible solutions to their problem. Some
people hear the word "bankruptcy" and become panicked.
They think "bankruptcy" is a crime instead of a federal law
designed to protect consumers. Others believe credit
counseling is the only legitimate option, but later learn it is

only limited to resolving credit card debt. Some people will try debt settlement and then shockingly discover that they have to pay taxes on the settled debt as "income", which I will explain in Chapter 4.

Without sufficient information and a willingness to trust someone when it comes to resolving a debt problem, many people do nothing. They hope the problem will simply disappear. Why? Because they have lost trust in the credit system. There's no doubt there are some charlatans in this country who take advantage of people struggling. Keep in mind though, that there are many legitimate and honest debt relief experts who can help. You just need to trust them.

> *"I started having nightmares because the phone would not stop ringing, and I would wake up every AM in tears. I found Kevin Heupel and I feel more like myself and I'm sleeping much better."*
>
> *-Barbara F.*

Emotional Hurdle #2: PERCEPTION

PERCEPTION: "Consciousness; quick, acute, and intuitive cognition" (Merriam-Webster's Collegiate Dictionary, Eleventh Edition)

Overcoming the emotional hurdle of perception requires you to face your worst enemy – YOU. For example, if you think bankruptcy is not an option, then you need to change your perception of bankruptcy and look at the positive aspects of getting help.

Many famous and successful people have filed for bankruptcy. Walt Disney and Sam Walton both filed bankruptcy. Were they failures? Heck, no! They rightfully perceived bankruptcy as a financial tool they could use to eliminate their debt and try again. Bankruptcy is a federal law and first enacted in the U.S. in 1800 by the second President of United States, John Adams. We should be thankful that we have a legal right to get out of debt. Bankruptcy allowed Walt Disney to bring great entertainment to our country. For Sam Walton, bankruptcy allowed him to build a business that forced companies to sell their products at affordable prices to all consumers.

Different people have different perceptions. As goes the saying: "What's one man's meat is another man's poison."

[4] It reminds me of the following story of a couple who bought a donkey from the market:

The Man, the Boy, and the Donkey[5]

A Man and his son were once going with their Donkey to market. As they were walking along by the donkey's side a countryman passed them and said: "You fools, what is a Donkey for but to ride upon?"

So the Man put the Boy on the Donkey and they went on their way. But soon they passed a group of men, one of whom said: "See that lazy youngster, he lets his father walk while he rides."

So the Man ordered his Boy to get off, and got on himself. But they hadn't gone far when they passed two women, one of whom said to the other: "Shame on that lazy lout to let his poor little son trudge along."

Well, the Man didn't know what to do, but at last he took his Boy up before him on the Donkey. By this time they had come to the town, and the passers-by began to jeer and point at them. The Man stopped and asked what they were scoffing at. The men said: "Aren't you ashamed of yourself for overloading that poor Donkey of yours—you and your hulking son?"

The Man and Boy got off and tried to think what to do. They thought and they thought, till at last they cut down a pole, tied the Donkey's feet to it, and raised the pole and the Donkey to their shoulders.

---

[4] German proverb
[5] Aesop's Fables; http://www.bartleby.com/17/1/62.html

They went along amid the laughter of all who met them till they came to Market Bridge, when the Donkey, getting one of his feet loose, kicked out and caused the Boy to drop his end of the pole. In the struggle the Donkey fell over the bridge, and his fore-feet being tied together he was drowned.

"That will teach you," said an old man who had followed them.

Having an incorrect perception of potential solutions results in bad decisions. You can never have everyone praise you, nor should you expect everyone to condemn you. When you are more concerned about what other people will think, you cannot make good decisions when it comes to getting out of debt.

I remember one client who had $200,000 in credit card debt from a failed business and $150,000 in retirement savings. This client cashed out his 401k at a 10% tax penalty and paid the $120,000 towards the $200,000 of credit card debt. The problem was that he still had $80,000 of credit card debt, which was too much to repay at his $60,000 annual salary. Worse yet, he created a tax problem as his withdrawal from his retirement account before the age of 59½ was taxable as ordinary income in addition to paying the 10% tax penalty. Draining his retirement savings did not solve his problem; it made it worse.

The client eventually filed for bankruptcy protection because he had no choice. What he should have done was file *prior* to cashing out his retirement savings. Why?

When you file for bankruptcy 100% of your retirement accounts are protected, which means you don't lose any of your retirement savings. Had this client initially filed bankruptcy, he would have wiped out $200,000 of debt, kept all of his retirement, *and* avoided a tax liability with the IRS. He didn't file bankruptcy because he didn't like the thought of how people would perceive him. By being more concerned people's opinions, he made a terrible financial decision for himself.

> *"I didn't think anyone was going to help me with my situation. My daughter was calling credit counseling and nobody would help. She saw Kevin Heupel on Colorado's Best and called for an appointment. And you helped me. Many thanks, now I don't have to worry anymore."*
>
> *-Gloria B.*

Emotional Hurdle #3: COURAGE

COURAGE: "Mental or moral strength to venture, persevere, and withstand danger, fear, or difficulty" (Merriam-Webster's Collegiate Dictionary, Eleventh Edition)

There is no doubt that our culture induces fear, even among those who have no cause to be afraid. One of the funniest stories about the effects of fear is from Dr. Jack Groppel, co-founder of the Human Performance Institute, who operates a training camp in Florida where business leaders, athletes, and law enforcement officers are trained in the skills they need to improve their performance. Dr. Groppel's story was about four tough football players, each standing over 6' 4" tall and weighing more than 350 pounds.

The four football players were told to run a mile in nine minutes – not a difficult challenge for men of their physical capabilities. When they reached the end of the mile they were to touch a white fence, and then run back to the training center. As they prepared for the run, Dr. Groppel told them to be aware that they would be running through a swampy area where they might encounter an alligator or two and might need to make a detour around them. But they had to be careful, in their detour, not to step on any poisonous snakes. As the runners were about to take off from the starting line, Dr. Groppel added, "Oh yes, I spotted a couple of wild boars wandering around the property last week. They are really aggressive and have really sharp tusk! If you see any of those, be sure and take appropriate action!" And off the players ran.

What the football players didn't know was that one of Dr. Groppel's assistants was waiting in bushes along the running trail. When the four huge football players passed his bush, he snorted like a pig and shook the branches. The four big, tough, football players all jumped, yelled like little children, and ran in the opposite direction as fast as they could go! Needless to say, they didn't complete the assignment of touching the white fence.

Fear does funny things to us. People will avoid dealing with their debt problem because they "fear" the outcome. They will avoid settling a tax debt with the IRS because they "fear" the IRS will take everything they own. This is simply not true. Every state has an exemption law that lets you keep certain assets, such as your home, even when you owe debts to a creditor including the IRS. For example, in Colorado, you can keep a home with $60,000 of equity without fear of a creditor taking and selling your home. In Arizona, the amount is $150,000 and it's unlimited in Florida.

Another fear people have is that they'll lose their retirement savings. But again, it's not true. What *is* true is if you don't pay your debts, your situation will get worse. Creditors can sue you, garnish your wages, and seize certain property. The fear people have about the potential solutions then become a reality if they don't do anything about resolving their debt problem.

Getting over fear requires courage. People have to get out of their comfort zone and reach out for help. Solving a debt problem requires being open to the possibility of solutions. More importantly, it requires seeking advise on the issue from an expert. Your family and friends are not equipped to advise you on filing for bankruptcy or entering into a debt settlement program. Their opinions are clouded by their own perceptions and they are not experts.

The best way to overcome fear about debt is to call a debt relief attorney. Most attorneys offer a free consultation to review your entire financial situation. They can explain the advantages and disadvantages of each potential solution. Meet with at least three attorneys to make sure you are getting consistent advice, and keep meeting with experts until you understand the best solution and have the courage to get started.

> *"It's been stressful trying to get through all the information about getting out of debt. After I met and talked with Kevin Heupel, who I felt was very patient with me, I felt less stressed and scared."*
>
> *-Marcia S.*

Emotional Hurdle #4: ACCEPTANCE

ACCEPTANCE: "An agreeing either expressly or by conduct to the offer of another" (Merriam-Webster's Collegiate Dictionary, Eleventh Edition)

Acceptance means embracing what is, rather than wishing for what is not. When we accept difficult realties, we are able to discover what may be possible to resolve the situation.

A great story about acceptance is the following:

The Law of the Garbage Truck[6]

One day I hopped in a taxi and we took off for the airport. We were driving in the right lane when suddenly a black car jumped out of a parking space right in front of us. My taxi driver slammed on his brakes, skidded, and missed the other car by just inches! The driver of the other car whipped his head around and started yelling at us.

My taxi driver just smiled and waved at the guy. And I mean he was really friendly. So I asked, "Why did you just do that? This guy almost ruined your car and sent us to the hospital!" This is when my taxi driver taught me what I now call, "The Law of the Garbage Truck."

---

[6] The Law of the Garbage Truck, D.J. Pollay, Sterling Publishing, 2012.

He explained that many people are like garbage trucks. They run around full of garbage, full of frustration, full of anger, and full of disappointment. As their garbage piles up, they need a place to dump it and sometimes they'll dump it on you. Don't take it personally. Just smile, wave, wish them well, and move on. Don't take their garbage and spread it to other people at work, at home, or on the streets. The bottom line is that successful people do not let garbage trucks take over their day. Life's too short to wake up in the morning with regrets. Life is ten percent what you make it and ninety percent how you take it.

Overcoming a debt problem requires "accepting" the reality of your financial situation. When you have unsecured debt (debt for which there is no direct collateral, such as a car or a house) that exceeds 20% of your gross income, you will never be able to repay the debt by making minimum payments due to compounding interest rates. You can only get out of overwhelming debt by "accepting" that bankruptcy or another debt solution is a reality.

You have to face the facts; even the best of us make mistakes. Not accepting the reality of your debt problem keeps you stuck and unable to live a productive life. You can't live in the present and plan for the future if your head and finances are stuck in the past. Nor can you waste energy being angry about creditors who won't work with you. "Resentment is like drinking poison and then hoping it will kill your enemies."(Nelson Mandela)

Life is just as it should be. Make the best out of any situation. You cannot change reality by wishing your debt problem had never happened. Accepting the reality of your situation and living fully within your reality facilitates letting go of the past and moving ahead to the future, a future you carve out for yourself based on what you want, not based on where you used to be. You have to take action and do something about the problem or the garbage truck will control your life.

"Thank you for all your help with our finances!! Our life is so much better. Something that you do daily has really made a difference in our lives, and we want to thank you and your staff."

-Tony & Diana T.

www.GetDebtFreeWithMe.com   (720) 443-4030

Emotional Hurdle #5: BELIEF

BELIEF: "A state or habit of mind in which trust or confidence is placed in some person or thing" (Merriam-Webster's Collegiate Dictionary, Eleventh Edition)

One of the first steps to achieving financial success is having belief in yourself. How many things have you not done or tried because you lacked that confidence? You have to believe you are doing the right thing for yourself and your family by getting out of debt. Believing in yourself is about being sure that you are doing what is right for you, regardless of what other people think. As Eleanor Roosevelt said, "No one can make you feel inferior without your consent."

Your friends and family will have their own opinions about bankruptcy, credit counseling, debt settlement, etc., but that is just their opinion—not based on fact and certainly not the truth. Your friends probably know less about bankruptcy than you do, especially if they have never struggled with debt. This fable does a good job of explaining how others can limit our beliefs and keep us trapped in our current situation:

The Fable of the Eagle and the Chicken[7]

A fable is told about an eagle who thought he was a chicken. When the eagle was very small, he fell

---

[7] Walk Tall, You're a Daughter of God, by Jamie Glenn. Deseret Book Company, 1994, pp. 22-4.

from the safety of his nest. A chicken farmer found the eagle, brought him to the farm, and raised him in a chicken coop among his many chickens. The eagle grew up doing what chickens do, living like a chicken, and believing he was a chicken.

A naturalist came to the chicken farm to see if what he had heard about an eagle acting like a chicken was really true. He knew that an eagle is king of the sky. He was surprised to see the eagle strutting around the chicken coop, pecking at the ground, and acting very much like a chicken. The farmer explained to the naturalist that this bird was no longer an eagle. He was now a chicken because he had been trained to be a chicken and he believed that he was a chicken.

The naturalist knew there was more to this great bird than his actions showed as he "pretended" to be a chicken. He was born an eagle and had the heart of an eagle, and nothing could change that. The man lifted the eagle onto the fence surrounding the chicken coop and said, "Eagle, thou art an eagle. Stretch forth thy wings and fly." The eagle moved slightly, only to look at the man; then he glanced down at his home among the chickens in the chicken coop where he was comfortable. He jumped off the fence and continued doing what chickens do. The farmer was satisfied. "I told you it was a chicken," he said.

The naturalist returned the next day and tried again to convince the farmer and the eagle that the eagle was born for something greater. He took the eagle to the top of the farmhouse and spoke to him: "Eagle, thou art an eagle. Thou dost belong to the sky and not to the earth. Stretch forth thy wings and fly." The large bird looked at the man, then again down into the chicken coop. He jumped from the man's arm onto the roof of the farmhouse.

Knowing what eagles are really about, the naturalist asked the farmer to let him try one more time. He would return the next day and prove that this bird was an eagle. The farmer, convinced otherwise, said, "It is a chicken."

The naturalist returned the next morning to the chicken farm and took the eagle and the farmer some distance away to the foot of a high mountain. They could not see the farm or the chicken coop from this new setting. The man held the eagle on his arm and pointed high into the sky where the bright sun was beckoning above. He spoke: "Eagle, thou art an eagle! Thou dost belong to the sky and not to the earth. Stretch forth thy wings and fly." This time the eagle stared skyward into the bright sun, straightened his large body, and stretched his massive wings. His wings moved, slowly at first, then surely and powerfully. With the mighty screech of an eagle, he flew.

Your level of self-belief isn't set in stone. We can all be flexible and change, even "fly" like an eagle when we think we're a chicken. When you start to doubt yourself, you are listening to that negative inner voice casting uncertainty. Whose voice is it: your parents', friends', some TV critic's? Some people think that unless everyone agrees with them, then they are doing the wrong thing. That thinking is self-

 www.GetDebtFreeWithMe.com   (720) 443-4030

destructive. Don't let others limit your possibilities for getting out of debt.

Stop thinking that other people's opinions are important and concentrate on what's best for you. You have to believe that you'll get out of debt.

"If you think you can, you can. And if you think you can't, you are right." (Henry Ford)

• • •

"You can tell Kevin Heupel cares about his clients. Very Helpful! Pleasure to deal with when already dealing with a stressful situation – he makes things a little easier."

-Nathaniel S.

• • •

Emotional Hurdle #6: FEAR

FEAR: "An unpleasant, often strong emotion caused by anticipation or awareness of danger" (Merriam-Webster's Collegiate Dictionary, Eleventh Edition)

Our discussion so far about the emotional hurdles for getting out of debt has all shared one central theme: FEAR. Fear affects the ability to Trust. Fear clouds your Perception of reality. To overcome Fear, you need Courage to Accept your reality and Believe in yourself.

There are many fears about dealing with debt problems:

- There is the fear of what will happen if you don't repay the debt, and the fear of what will happen if you do.
- There is fear about the consequences of credit counseling, bankruptcy, debt settlement, and other solutions.
- There is the fear of doing nothing.
- There is fear of getting sued and having your wages garnished.
- There is also the fear of friends' and family's reactions to learning about your debt problem.

All of these fears are magnified by a lack of knowledge about the options.

No one wants to feel judged or rejected, but there is no reason to live in "fear" of other people's opinions. Nothing others do is because of you; what they say and do is a projection of their own reality. When you are immune to the opinions and actions of others, you won't be the victim of needless suffering. The best way to overcome this fear is to educate yourself about your options. This book provides the information you need to evaluate your choices, as well as advice on what approach is appropriate in which situation.

Clients constantly ask me if bankruptcy is a matter of public record because they fear how people will react and treat them. Yes, bankruptcy is a matter of public record, and there are some newspapers that will print the names of people who file bankruptcy, but this will be in the back of the newspaper, under Public Notices, that few people read.

Regardless of whether your bankruptcy is discovered in this way, I recommend my clients tell their family and friends about it. You would be surprised by how many people will be eager to support you emotionally as you go through the process. This turns out to be the case even when your friends and family did not think bankruptcy was a good idea.

Don't expect everyone to support you though. One of my clients lost a friend of sixteen years after filing bankruptcy because the "so-called friend" felt she couldn't associate with someone who didn't pay her debts. Losing a friend after struggling with debt is painful, but it's worse to remain in a debt situation that will only get worse. Regardless of what decision you make, going through a difficult process like bankruptcy reveals your true friends and supporters.

Fear is a fact of life. It is part of the range of feelings that humans experience on a daily basis. In our culture, fear has come to be viewed as a negative; however, fear is a perfectly normal feeling. We would all feel a lot better if we simply allowed ourselves to experience it fully and then do something about it.

When it comes to getting out of debt, fear leads to panic and confusion. People start to worry how they can "save face" due to the fear they are feeling over not repaying their debts. Fear triggers avoidance of the facts and makes people want to stop searching for a debt relief solution. But fear is a creation of our own minds as portrayed in this Cherokee Legend:

Two Wolves[8]

One evening an old Cherokee told his grandson about a battle that goes on inside people.

He said, "My son, the battle is between two wolves inside us all.

"One is Evil – It is anger, envy, jealousy, sorrow, regret, greed, arrogance, self-pity, guilt, resentment, inferiority, lies, false pride, superiority, and ego.

---

[8] http://www.firstpeople.us/FP-Html-Legends/TwoWolves-Cherokee.html

"The other is Good – It is joy, peace, love, hope, serenity, humility, kindness, benevolence, empathy, generosity, truth, compassion and faith."

The grandson thought about it for a minute and then asked his grandfather: "Which wolf wins?"

The old Cherokee simply replied, "The one you feed."

The antidote to fear is truth. You always have a choice about how to respond and deal with fear. You can give into it, struggle with it, accept it, or work around it. To make the right choice, you need to get to the truth of your situation and find out what will solve your debt problem. With truth and an action plan, your fears will subside.

The remainder of this book will discuss the most common solutions to debt problems and calm your fears about getting out of debt.

> *"Kevin Heupel has been very helpful in this process. The overwhelming procedure of being over my head financially has been very stressful. In times of financial burden, it is good to know there is a law firm that would help me. I am grateful that I found Kevin Heupel and plan to recommend his company as often as possible."*
>
> *- Linda C.*

CHAPTER TWO: Popular Debt Solutions

There are a lot of books about finances and debt. Two authors I like are Dave Ramsey and Suze Orman. I think they do a great job of explaining how we need to save money, live within a budget, and contribute towards our retirement. Both have simple and common-sense solutions that are easy to follow when it comes to building wealth. I don't think they do a good job when it comes to explaining how to get out of debt though.

Recently, on Oprah.com, Suze Orman published the following Q&A[9]:

> Q: After taking out cash advances on her credit cards, my 81-year-old mother is out $8,000. She lives on $600 a month from Social Security and cannot keep paying on this debt. Can you advise me on how to proceed? How do I get her out of credit card debt?
>
> **A:** As daunting as an $8,000 debt looks, I'm relieved the figure isn't higher, given your mother's generous nature. A cash advance on a credit card is one of the worst types of borrowing because the interest rate is typically 21 percent or more. It's fruitless to try to talk your way out of this; the card issuer has every right to expect repayment.

---

[9] http://www.oprah.com/money/Suze-Orman-Debt-Advice-How-to-Get-Out-of-Debt

To regain control of her debt, have your mom keep paying at least the minimum due on the monthly credit card bill. On-time installments are vital for protecting her FICO credit rating. That's important because if her score is at least 700, she has a good chance of being able to transfer the entire balance to a new card with a lower interest rate. Many card issuers offer zero percent interest for the first year when you move your balance to their card. At CardTrak.com, click on Credit Cards, then choose Balance Transfer to find issuers offering the best deals. But only sign up for one card—multiple applications made at the same time can actually hurt her credit score.

The problem with the answer above is that it assumes the mother can qualify for a 0% interest credit card, which I highly doubt. The mother receives $7,200 per year from Social Security, but has $8,000 of debt. The mother needs all of her income just to buy food, utilities, and other basic necessities. Making the minimum payments on the credit cards is making it harder for her to live. I doubt the mother will qualify for a credit card at 0% interest because her debt-to-income ratio is out of whack. When unsecured debt (credit cards, medical bills, payday loans, lines of credit, personal loans, student loans, taxes; everything except a car loan and mortgage) exceed 20% of your annual income, it is a sign of financial distress so don't plan on refinancing debt as a solution.

Dave Ramsey promotes what he calls his "Debt Snowball Plan." The principle is that you stop everything except minimum payments and focus on one debt at a time. Otherwise, nothing gets accomplished because your effort is diluted. First, he wants you to accumulate $1,000 cash as an emergency fund. Then you list your debts, beginning with the debt with the lowest payoff or balance, regardless of the interest rate. If you have two debts with a similar balance, then list the one with the higher interest rate first. Your goal, according to Ramsey, is to pay the small debt first so you get a quick sense of accomplishment and stay motivated. You attack the smallest debt first while maintaining minimum payments on everything else.

Similar to Orman's recommendation, the Debt Snowball Plan does not take into consideration the amount of debt you are carrying relative to your annual income. Ramsey assumes that one has enough disposable income to pay towards the debt, but the reality is that most people who are struggling with debt do not have excess funds.

The premise for my book is not to attack or counter the financial advice of Ramsey or Orman. They have terrific advice for building a strong financial future. I actually follow a lot of Dave Ramsey's advice when it comes to college savings, retirement, and mortgages. But they lack the understanding that sometimes people have too much debt and need to resolve that problem before they can save money.

I believe the best financial plan is one that gets you out of debt as quickly as possible. This means, in some cases, not repaying all of your debts. This shocks many people as we feel obligated to honor our debts; however, sometimes we have too much debt to repay.

People feel guilty about not repaying their debts. It's an emotionally challenge. I get it and it's a sign of good character because it means you're not trying to cheat your creditors. However, people need to come to terms with the fact that "paying off your debt" is not always realistic. It is better to find a solution that allows one to start saving towards retirement today instead of continuing to pay off old debts.

In this chapter, I briefly describe the most popular debt solutions. I devote subsequent chapters to each solution and explain them in detail. The most popular and legitimate solutions to resolving debt problems are:

> (1) Credit Counseling;
>
> (2) Debt Settlement;
>
> (3) Bankruptcy;
>
> (4) Loan Modification;
>
> (5) Offer in Compromise; and
>
> (6) Student Loan Repayment Options.

Credit Counseling: Credit counseling is handled by non-profit groups that consolidate credit card debt over the course of a five year-period at a lower interest rate than what each individual credit card currently charges. Credit counseling works if your <u>only</u> debt is credit card debt. It does not work if your debt consists of medical bills, judgments against your property or car, personal loans, lines of credit, or other types of debt. For more information on credit counseling, see Chapter 3.

Debt Settlement: Debt settlement involves settling debt for 20 to 50 cents on the dollar and the rest of the money gets written off. For example, if you have $50,000 of debt, you can realistically expect to settle the debt for $20,000. Debt Settlement is a solution that is heavily advertised as an alternative to bankruptcy. It can work for most credit unsecured debts like card debts, medical bills, judgments, etc. I explain this process in greater detail in Chapter 4.

Bankruptcy: Bankruptcy is a federal law and has been a legal way to erase debt in the United States for over 200 years. Popular bankruptcy options include Chapters 7, 11, and 13. Bankruptcy protection gives every American a legal right to get out of debt. Even Dave Ramsey filed bankruptcy about twenty years ago.

Federal bankruptcy laws have their origins from the Bible. Nehemiah 10:31b[10] states:

> "Every seven years we will let our fields rest, and we will cancel all debts."

---

[10] https://www.bible.com/bible/392/neh.10.cevus06

The irony about bankruptcy is that people think it's a crime or a dishonorable thing to do; however, it's your legal right to get out of debt. As we'll discuss in Chapter 5, bankruptcy is often the best solution as it provides the most predictable way for solving a debt problem.

Loan Modification: A loan modification involves a homeowner asking his mortgage company to reorganize his payments so that the monthly mortgage payment is less than 31% of his gross monthly income. Loan modifications became an option a few years ago when President Obama created the Home Affordable Modification Program (HAMP). The objective of HAMP was to stem the rising tide of foreclosures and keep people in their homes. This federal program has not been a great success, though it did encourage lenders to start modifying mortgages on their own. A loan modification is a great way to reduce your monthly mortgage payment and may provide excess funds in your budget to pay other debts. Chapter 6 will explore loan modifications in greater detail.

Offer in Compromise: An offer in compromise is a process conducted through the Internal Revenue Service that allows taxpayers to settle their outstanding tax debts for pennies on the dollar. It is similar to debt settlement; however, an offer in compromise is a formal process and the IRS uses a specific formula to determine whether you're insolvent. The IRS generally approves an offer in compromise when the amount offered represents the most the IRS can expect to collect within a reasonable period of time. I explain this in greater detail in Chapter 7.

Student Loans: There are several options for reducing your monthly payments for student loans and eliminating unpaid balances. Unfortunately, many people don't know about these programs, which are offered through the U.S. Department of Education. Anyone with a student loan can lower their monthly payments. You don't have to be in financial distress. There are some repayment plans that base the payment on a percentage of your gross monthly income. Other programs will forgive the outstanding balance after so many years of repaying your student loans. I explain all of the options in greater detail in Chapter 8.

How do I know if I have too much debt?
The biggest question I get is "when someone should look towards these solutions?" Or, "how do I know if I have too much debt?" There are two indicators: the obvious and not-so-obvious signs.

The obvious signs of a debt problem are when you start missing payments, you don't have enough money to pay your credit card so you skip the payment, or you are 30-60 days late on your car loan or mortgage. Another obvious sign is that you are getting collection calls. If you are receiving letters from attorneys or have been sued for an old debt, then it's certainly a sign of a debt problem. The most obvious sign is when your wages and bank accounts are being garnished. Most states allow a creditor to garnish 25% of your wages to repay a judgment debt. That is a high percentage to disappear from your paycheck or bank account; and if you're already struggling to pay your bills, a garnishment will make life much harder to manage.

Another indicator is credit score dropping below 700. Creditors look at your credit score as a way to gauge the likelihood of your credit-worthiness and future ability to repay a debt. A score above 700 is a sign of stability. More importantly, it allows you to qualify for the best interest rates when you buy a car or home. When your score drops below 700, it is the first sign that your future ability to repay may be impacted. Creditors will still loan you money, but at a higher interest rate.

A not-so-obvious sign is your own mental state. Do you dream of getting an inheritance or winning the lottery (I mean, more than the rest of us)? Do you wish you could find money hidden somewhere or fantasize about stealing it without getting caught? Worse yet, do you wish you were dead so that your life insurance could pay off your debt? If you're having unrealistic thoughts about getting out of debt, it is time to look at one of the above solutions.

The final test is the amount of unsecured debt you are carrying relative to your annual income. If your unsecured debt exceeds 20% of your annual gross income, it is sign of financial distress. The percentage surprises people because if you think about someone earning $30,000 per year, his unsecured debt needs to be below $6,000 for him to be in a secure financial state. If he has more than $6,000 of unsecured debt, then he has a debt problem.

Why is 20% a sign of financial distress? In June 1999, the American Bankruptcy Institute Journal published an article that looked at similarities among people who had filed for bankruptcy in 1997. The common theme was that unsecured debt at the time of bankruptcy exceeded 20% of gross income. Think about it: we need most of our income to support a lifestyle equivalent to our income. This includes buying food, making car payments, paying taxes, and covering the other necessities of life. Once debt accumulates above 20%, it competes against your food budget, makes it harder to afford a reliable car, and alters your life choices.

Does this mean that you need to immediately file for bankruptcy or begin a credit counseling course if your debts are greater than 20%? Maybe – but it's not an absolute rule. Some people have higher incomes, but live a modest lifestyle so they can afford to have a higher amount of debt. Others might have student loan debt that represents 40% of their gross annual income, but are on an income-based repayment plan where their payment does not exceed 10% of their gross monthly income. There are always exceptions to the rule.

The final sign of financial distress is how long it will take you to repay your debts. Credit card statements show how many years it will take you to pay off your balance. For example, if you make your monthly minimum payment, the box may state that it will take 20-25 years to pay off the debt. If you increase your payment five-fold, you can reduce the payoff term from twenty to seven years. This information provides insight as to whether you can afford to repay your debt. As a rule of thumb, if you cannot pay off your debt within five years, then it's too much and you need help.

I use the five-year rule because credit counseling and Chapter 13 bankruptcy allow you to repay debts over a five year period. After five years, whatever is not paid is forgiven in a Chapter 13. It's similar to the Bible where after seven years your debts should be forgiven. Thus, if it will take you more than five years to pay off a debt, then it's time to find a debt relief solution.

> *"After a long hard 4 years I finally found Heupel Law. With their help, I'll enjoy my senior years stress free. They have helped me make the worst time of my life easier to go through in a timely fashion. Heupel Law was there for me."*
>
> *-Verneice W.*

CHAPTER THREE: Credit Counseling

Credit counseling became popular after 2005 when Congress required people who were considering bankruptcy to take a credit counseling class to learn how to budget. Credit counseling involves combining all of your credit cards into a single payment at a lower interest rate than what the individual card is charging. The goal is to repay the credit card debt within five years. This works well if your only debt is credit cards. It does not work if your debt consists of medical bills, judgments, personal loans, lines of credit, student loans, or other types of debt. Credit counseling helps consumers by negotiating with the credit card company to agree for a new repayment plan.

When consumers contact a credit counseling agency, they are typically offered a counseling session in which they share information about their income, expenses, and debts. As a result of that consultation, they may be offered a Debt Management Plan or DMP.

The best thing about credit counseling is that it creates a DMP that requires you to make only a single payment at a reduced interest rate. Most plans involve repaying your debt over a 3-5 year period. Given the short repayment period, the monthly payment is substantially higher than the current minimum payments, even though the interest rate is lower, because the repayment is accelerated by the shorter time period. Under credit counseling, you are still expected to repay the full amount of your debt.

Credit counseling stops collection calls once your program is established. It also avoids your debt being "charged off," which would negatively affect your credit score, and sold to a collection company that would most likely sue you for the debt and garnish your wages. This protection from collections will extend throughout the entire repayment period.

Credit counseling is reported to your credit report. Accounts included in that plan are usually noted as "not being paid as agreed." Creditors may also report that the payments are being received through a credit counseling service. The credit counseling companies will tell you this is a good sign because it shows you are dedicated to paying your debts. However, it is very difficult to qualify for new credit until you have completed two years of payments under this plan. While under the Fair Credit Reporting Act, a negative item, such as "account not being paid as agreed", remains on your credit report for seven years from the date it was first reported, but it does not negatively impact your credit score.

There is no reduction of the outstanding balances when you enter a credit counseling program, though you can have late and over-limit fees removed. The other thing to be aware of is that once you enter credit counseling, you can no longer use the credit cards for upcoming purchases. Your existing credit cards will be suspended or closed to new charges. Therefore, if you want to purchase a car or buy a home while in credit counseling, it may not be possible.

Credit counseling is not for everyone. If you're currently struggling to make the minimum payments on your credit cards, then credit counseling programs will be too expensive.

If you are considering signing up with a credit counseling service, there are a few things you need to know. First, credit counseling firms can charge high service fees, even if they advertise they are non-profit organizations. These fees can be in the hundreds or even thousands of dollars, and some want an upfront payment before they will help you. Additionally, such services usually charge a monthly fee that is not applied against your debt. Even though the credit counseling service goes through the process of negotiating your interest rates at the beginning of the debt management plan, after that, they don't do much work. They simply take your payments every month, and then make your payments to the credit card companies for you. For this, you might have to pay a service fee of $30 to $50 per month, which does not include the amount you must pay to the creditors in the debt management plan.

A common complaint about credit counseling services is that some don't make the consumer's payments on time. This results not only in late fees, but also results in a damaged credit rating. Thus, you have to do your homework before choosing a credit counseling company.

As with any purchase, shop around for the best program. Look at credit counseling agencies that have been approved by the U.S. Department of Justice to provide the credit counseling classes for those considering bankruptcy. This way, you will know you are dealing with a reputable company even if you don't plan to file for bankruptcy. Many approved credit counseling agencies provide counseling services in languages other than English. For a list of approved agencies and languages, go to http://www.justice.gov/ust/eo/bapcpa/ccde/cc_approved .htm. Be sure to check out the service with the Better Business Bureau to learn about any complaints and whether those complaints were resolved.

Little is known about the success of credit counseling. According to Gail Cunningham, vice president of public relations for the National Foundation for Credit Counseling (NFCC), 53% of consumers who enter a formal DMP either complete it or notify the counselor that they are financially stable enough to resume paying their bills independently. This means that 47% of consumers drop out of the program. A recent survey by Cambridge Credit Counseling found that only one in five of its inquiries actually resulted in debt management enrollment.

According to Cambridge Credit Counseling's Transparency Project's 2010 results:

- After a comprehensive credit review, counselors recommended a DMP to just over one-third (34%)

of consumers. Just under one-quarter (23%) of consumers enrolled in a DMP.

- Of those who enrolled in a DMP, the typical Cambridge client received an interest rate reduction from 21.62% to 7.96%, resulting in an average saving of $181.86 in interest charges per month. Payments were reduced, on average, by $192.70.

- In 2010, Cambridge clients who completed their DMP had done so in an average of 41 months. Fees were waived or reduced for about 27% of clients. Creditors also paid the agency an average of $12.32 per account per payment in what is called "Fair Share." This involves paying the credit cards on a prorated basis. For example, if you have two debts – one for $2000 and the other for $8000, the $8000 debt will receive 80% of the payment.

- Overall client satisfaction was 97.9% for new clients and 96.7% for existing clients.

- At the 6-month mark, 75.9% of Cambridge Credit Counseling clients said they had reviewed or revised their budgets, 62.4% were tracking expenses, and 27.7% were building savings.

Despite these positive numbers, just under one-quarter of consumers who contacted this credit counseling agency enrolled in a DMP. Not all clients who enroll in a DMP complete it either. Some drop out for positive reasons, such as getting back on track or paying off their remaining debt more quickly, while others drop out for negative reasons, such as not being able to keep up with their payments or decided to file for bankruptcy. Cambridge reported losing 16.7% of its DMP client base in 2010.

The most important thing about credit counseling is to make sure you can afford the program. I've had several clients over the years who enrolled in credit counseling for one to two years, but later had to file for bankruptcy. As a result, they wasted a lot of money being in the program due to their false pride at avoiding bankruptcy.

One client was in a credit counseling program for 24 months and paid $1,000 per month. Her total credit card debt was around $60,000 before enrolling in the program, and she was struggling to make the minimum payments at the time she started. After she enrolled, her payments increased due to the accelerated payment schedule, and when she couldn't make the new monthly payment, she withdrew money from her retirement account. It was only once the retirement money was gone and she could no longer afford the monthly credit counseling payment that she came to see me.

She decided to file for bankruptcy as it was her best option; it eliminated the remaining credit card balances and got her completely out of debt. However, if she had seen me prior to entering credit counseling, I could have saved her $24,000 in credit counseling payments as well as kept her from depleting her entire retirement savings. I'm not promoting bankruptcy over credit counseling, but in her case, her perception about bankruptcy and credit counseling was mistaken. As a result, she made the wrong decision. Had she met with a debt relief attorney prior to enrolling in credit counseling, she would have been fully informed, and hopefully, made a wiser financial decision rather than one based on fear.

> *"Kevin Heupel has been extremely helpful to me. I live on a fixed income which makes for a very tight financial situation. He made sure I understood the process and made me very comfortable talking to him."*
>
> *-Anne V.*

Summary of Credit Counseling Pros and Cons

PROS	CONS
You make only one payment with substantially lower interest rates.	Credit counseling only applies to credit card debt.
Your credit score is not negatively impacted while in credit counseling.	The credit card debt must be repaid in full within five years.
Creditors cannot harass or sue you while you're in the program.	Credit counseling is not an option if you have other types of debts (e.g.; medical bills, personal loans, judgments, etc.).
	Credit counseling is not affordable if you are already struggling to make the minimum credit card payments.
	You cannot use your credit cards until the program is completed.
	There are monthly fees paid to the agency.

NOTES

_____

_____

_____

_____

_____

_____

_____

_____

_____

_____

_____

_____

_____

_____

_____

www.GetDebtFreeWithMe.com (720) 443-4030

CHAPTER FOUR: Debt Settlement

Debt settlement is a process wherein the debtor (the person who owes the debt) and the creditor (the person from whom the debtor has borrowed the money) come to a mutual agreement where the debtor agrees to pay part of the total sum he owes the creditor instead of the entire outstanding amount.

Debt settlement is heavily advertised as an alternative to bankruptcy. Settling your debt is certainly one way to get out of debt. After all, your creditors would prefer to get something rather than nothing so they're likely to work out a settlement with you. If you are willing to face the costs and nuances involved, then this could be the right solution for you.

With debt settlement arrangements, much of your outstanding debt is forgiven through negotiations. Many times a creditor is willing to accept less than the full amount: 20-50% of the outstanding balance. For example, if you have $50,000 of debt, you can realistically expect to settle the debt for $20,000. That's great, but there are some caveats.

Many people get excited about debt settlement because it is a way to pay off their debt at a lower cost. However, debt settlement doesn't work for most people struggling to pay their bills. If you are leaning towards settling your debt, then make sure you understand what it entails.

Before debt settlement can begin, the debt needs to be sold to a collection company because the original creditor will rarely, if ever, settle for less than is owed. Suppose you owe $10,000 on a credit card issued by Chase Bank and you hope to settle the debt for $2,000. Chase Bank has no interest in debt settlement because Chase already gives you the option of making a minimum payment each month. It is in Chase's best interest for you to continue making the minimum payment until the debt is paid as Chase makes more money from the interest it charges on the balance than having the debt paid in full.

If that's the case, how does the debt get to a collection agency? You have to stop making the minimum payment. As long you make your monthly payment, Chase is happy. To have your debt "sold" or transferred to a collection company, you need to stop making payments. After three to six months of missed payments, a bank like Chase will "charge off" the debt from your credit report.

Some people think a "charge off" is a good thing. When the debt is shown as "charged off" on a credit report, the balance is typically reported as zero. However, this doesn't mean that the debt is gone or forgiven. It simply means that Chase sold the debt to a collection company who now holds the note, which allows the new company to pursue collection of the entire debt.

When large banks sell debts to collection companies, the debt is sold at a reduced price. The amount is hard to predict as it depends on the package of debts being sold and the associated risks. Regardless of the actual amount, it is always sold for less than the actual face value of what is owed. Collection companies buy these debts in volume as they know some debts won't be collected, but a good majority of them will be paid. Credit cards are not limited to collecting only the amount they paid for the debt. They can collect the full amount owed including interest. Collection companies have cunning collection practices that induce people to pay. The best example is the collection company calls and tells you about your moral obligation to pay your debts and only criminals avoid repaying. The collection company wants you to feel ashamed and tricks you into thinking if you pay something, then you'll feel better about yourself. Remember though, the collection company is just trying to collect any sum of money and doesn't care about your emotional well-being.

Once the debt is sold to a collection company, you have a chance to settle the debt for less than what is owed. I use the 20-50% range because you don't know how much the collection company paid for the debt. If the debt was recently purchased, then 50% is a good target. Older debts may be settled for less, but you need the passage of time to help you lower the settlement amount.

However, there are problems with waiting for the debt to "age" in order to negotiate a reduced settlement. First, your credit score will take a huge hit. When a debt is "charged off", it results in a 40-60 point drop in your credit score. If the collection company notes they hold the debt in your credit report, instead of the bank that issued your credit card, that notation further reduces your score. In order to settle a debt, you have to be willing to sacrifice your credit score.

Negative posts remain on your credit record for seven years. That is a long time to wait if you need to buy a car. You may still get credit, but the interest rate will be much higher. If, however, there are too many "charge offs" on your credit report, you may not get credit at all.

Even when you settle a debt, the debt will appear on your credit report as having been settled for less than the full amount. This still hurts your credit score because potential lenders are reluctant to lend you money. It makes them worry you won't pay them back in full either. How much settling a debt hurts your score depends on your particular credit history, but it will definitely have a negative impact. If you're planning to take a loan in the near future, settling a debt probably isn't a good idea.

The negative effects on one's credit makes debt settlement an unattractive option, especially if your debt is primarily credit card debt. You would be better off in credit counseling as that does not negatively impact your credit score.

I find debt settlement to be useful for trade accounts. A trade account is a debt that is not listed on your credit report and typically recorded as an account payable. These include utility, medical, lawyer bills, and other service-related bills. These debts can age without dropping your credit score. As time goes by, the original creditor will be happy to get something instead of nothing.

When a debt is ready to be settled, all of the money needs to be available to make a lump sum payment. As you can imagine, creditors who are willing to accept $2,000 to resolve a $10,000 debt want their $2,000 at once; otherwise, it is not in their interest to reduce the principal balance. There are no payment plans for debt settlement because you have already shown that you cannot make payments in the first place. If you cannot pay the $2,000 in a lump sum and can only make payments, then the creditor will still expect to be paid the entire $10,000 even if it is a "charged off" debt.

The lump sum payment requirement makes debt settlement very difficult. Most people struggling with debt do not have large sums of cash; if they did, they would still be making payments to the original creditor. You certainly do not want to use every last penny of your savings to settle a debt if it won't resolve your entire debt problem. However, if you have an asset that you are willing to sell, then you can use the proceeds to pay off the debt.

Another surprise about debt settlement is the tax consequence. That's right – there are tax consequences when you settle a debt. Any amount of debt over $600 that is forgiven is considered "income" by the Internal Revenue Service. The amount forgiven will be reported on IRS form 1099. For example, if a creditor agrees to forgive

$8,000 on a debt, and you fall in the 25% income tax bracket, then you will owe $2,000 in additional taxes. And if you sold an asset to pay off the debt, you might also have to pay capital gains on the sale.

Sometimes debt settlement can turn a debt problem into a tax problem. You need to know where your income falls in your particular tax bracket. If your normal annual income is already in the upper part of your particular tax bracket, the amount forgiven could push you into the next higher bracket. That would result in higher taxes owed on all of your income from employment just because you settled a debt. The end result is that you may not have saved any money on the debt.

There are certainly some advantages to debt settlement. For one, you can be completely free of debt within 24 to 36 months. As mentioned above, your credit will take a hit so you need to take steps immediately in order to rebuild it.

One way to rebuild your credit is to have your creditors re-age your accounts and bring them to a current status in order to boost your credit score right away. Make this part of your negotiations, especially since your credit is probably not in good standing at this point. You can also negotiate to have the collection companies remove their listings from your credit report. Removing collection notations from your report will also boost your credit score and will help more than re-aging the original account.

For the peace of mind that comes with settling debts, there are tradeoffs. There's no easy way to release you from debt, and there is always a cost to dealing with a third party in the debt industry. With debt settlement, your chance of success is dependent upon the collection company's willingness to settle and at what price.

Debt settlement is not a universal tool that can be applied in all debt situations. Debt settlement cannot be used to help pay off a car loan, mortgage or other debt secured by collateral. It only works for unsecured debts, such as "charged off" credit cards, medical bills, payday loans, utility services, and other debts. If you are "upside down" or "underwater" on a car loan, meaning that you owe more than the car is worth, you cannot expect the bank to lower the balance to match the car's value. However, if your car was repossessed and the bank is trying to collect the deficiency balance, then the loan has become an unsecured debt that you can try to settle through debt settlement.

Mortgages are like car loans, and typically cannot be reduced through debt settlement. I say "typically" because the recent recession changed the rules. Over the last couple of years, my firm has had some success in removing second mortgages through debt settlement.

During the recent housing crisis, some homeowners found themselves in a situation where the value of their home was worth less than the balance of their first mortgage. For example, assume you own a home worth $195,000, hold a first mortgage of $200,000, and a second mortgage of $50,000. Although it is a secured debt, the second mortgage is like an unsecured loan because the value of the home is "underwater" and there is not enough equity to pay off the first mortgage. If the home were to go into foreclosure, the first mortgage company would receive all of the proceeds and the second mortgage company would receive nothing.

In these situations, I would approach the second mortgage holder and offer a lump sum payment in order to remove the deed of trust. Some mortgage companies are willing to settle for as little as 5% of the outstanding balance. In the above example, the homeowner could pay $2,500 to have the second mortgage removed from the property. That would represent a savings of $47,500. Keep in mind you would be liable for taxes on the settled amount so the savings are actually lower. With foreclosures on the decline and a rebound in housing prices, this strategy is starting to disappear and may not be an option in the foreseeable future.

Debt settlement takes time and can be a frustrating process. There are several debt settlement companies willing to assist. A quality consumer debt settlement firm will help you settle with creditors so that you only pay a portion of what is actually owed.

The typical debt settlement company will have you immediately stop paying your debts and start making a monthly payment to them. The monthly payment is used to create a fund, which can be used to settle the debts. Instead of paying $500 month to your outstanding debtors, you'll pay that amount to the debt settlement company who will hold the money in escrow to negotiate a lump sum payment. Within one year, you would have accumulated $6,000 in which to settle your debt.

A benefit of using a debt settlement company is the fact that the company handles the actual negotiations for you. Debt settlements require a lot of back and forth between the creditor and the debtor. A debt settlement company has extensive experience in these sometimes touchy negotiations.

However, debt settlement companies often charge upfront fee plus a monthly fee. More importantly, a debt settlement company will wait to pay your creditors when enough money has accumulated in your settlement account. While you may end up paying less to your creditor, you'll also be paying your debt settlement company so not all your money goes to the creditors.

Not all the creditors are willing to settle delinquent debts. Some may even treat you more harshly if you use such third party services. Some of my clients who hired debt settlement companies got sued more quickly than someone who did not use a debt settlement company because collection companies, knowing that debt settlement companies charge high fees, viewed the hiring of a debt settlement company as a sign of disposable income that could be used to pay their debt. As a result, the collection companies will file a lawsuit so they can get a judgment against you and start garnishing 25% of your wages.

Another problem with debt settlement companies is that working with one does not stop the collection efforts of creditors. Even though you are making monthly payments to settle your debts, collection companies are free to pursue their own collection efforts. If one of your objectives in hiring a debt settlement company is to avoid harassment from creditors, you'll find debt settlement to be very frustrating and disappointing.

Sometimes you hear about debt consolidation, which is not the same as debt settlement. Debt settlement reduces the amount of your debt, while debt consolidation reduces the number of creditors. In debt consolidation, you take out a new loan to pay off the ones you already have. Your new loan will likely have a lower interest rate than what you were paying on the other loans and your financial situation each month may be greatly simplified. Debt consolidation is similar to credit counseling, but goes beyond just repaying credit cards. It works if you still have good credit, but if not, debt settlement is the better option.

Debt settlement can play on the emotions of getting out of debt. Though it may seem an easy process, there are quite a few "ifs" and "buts" that come into play and make it tedious. The biggest problem is the fact that none of the creditors may be willing to forego the money you owe him, which will cause you to doubt the process. You will have to go through a series of debt negotiation meetings for the settlement process to work, which can make you fearful that the creditor will not settle with you.

Debt settlement companies can be helpful, but their services come at a price. You have to trust that they'll do their job and be successful. The entire process falls into place only once both parties come to common terms. That takes time and requires a lot of courageous effort. The interplay of emotions is common so understanding the "roller coaster" of getting out of debt is the key to anyone who considers debt settlement as a solution.

> *"I want you to know how much I appreciate all your help and your concern over the past few months. I know I've been a pest at times but you always helped. Kevin Heupel is such a great guy and such a professional. I haven't hesitated to recommend the firm to anyone who might be needing help.*
>
> *-Mary S.*

Summary of Debt Settlement Pros and Cons

PROS	CONS
You can settle the debt for pennies on the dollar.	This option is not available until after the debt is sold to a collection agency.
It's a good alternative to bankruptcy when you have too many "un-exempt" assets.	Applies to unsecured debt only – does not help to reduce mortgage or car payments.
Works best for trade accounts (i.e.; medical bills, attorney fees, and other debts not listed on your credit report).	No payment plans are available – you have to make a lump-sum payment.
	You pay income tax on the amount of settled debt.
	Debt settlement negatively impacts your credit score for 7 years after the "charge off".
	There are no rules and you have no control of the process – you are at the mercy of the collection company.
	Be cautious of debt settlement companies and their fees, as there are no guarantees of success.
	Debt settlement does not stop collection efforts or lawsuits.

NOTES

_____

_____

_____

_____

_____

_____

_____

_____

_____

_____

_____

_____

_____

_____

_____

_____

_____

CHAPTER FIVE: Bankruptcy

One of the best strategies for getting out of debt is filing for bankruptcy protection. People are surprised when I make this statement. Many people think bankruptcy is a crime. Collection companies and debt settlement agencies do a good job of perpetuating the myth that, somehow, filing for bankruptcy is dishonorable. Many books will say you should only file bankruptcy as a "last resort". Unfortunately, most of the pundits pushing that advice know nothing about bankruptcy.

What most people forget is that bankruptcy is a federal law first enacted by Congress in 1800 and signed by the second President of U.S., John Adams. <u>Every American has a legal right to get out of debt under the bankruptcy laws</u>. The notion of bankruptcy is not new or unique to the United States. In fact, the idea of bankruptcy has existed for thousands of years.

The federal bankruptcy law has its origins from the Bible and is referenced a couple of times. The first is in Nehemiah 10:31b, which states:

> "Every seven years we will let our fields rest, and we will cancel all debts."

The second reference is in Deuteronomy 15:1-2:

> "At the end of every seventh year you must cancel your debts. This is how it must be done. Creditors must cancel the loans they have made to their fellow Israelites. They must not demand payment

from their neighbors or relatives, for the Lord's time of release has arrived."

Filing for bankruptcy is a decision that requires serious thought, knowledge, and weighing your options. Obviously, detailed knowledge of the law is required to decide whether bankruptcy is your best option.

There are three common types of bankruptcy: Chapter 7, Chapter 11, and Chapter 13. Knowing which one to file depends upon your income, assets, and types of debts.

Chapter 7

A Chapter 7 bankruptcy is the most common bankruptcy filed. Chapter 7 eliminates most debts such as credit cards, medical bills, judgments, mortgage deficiencies, collection accounts, and many other debts. The elimination of debt through bankruptcy is called a "discharge," which means you are no longer obligated to pay the debt. Filing Chapter 7 bankruptcy eliminates all debts except student loans, child support, overdue taxes from the past three years, and court-ordered restitution. The biggest benefit of filing Chapter 7 is that it only takes 90 days to finish. It's one of the quickest debt relief options available.

Chapter 7 is known as a "liquidation nankruptcy" because the bankruptcy court appoints a "trustee" who can sell or "liquidate" your unprotected assets and use the sale proceeds to pay your creditors.

The nice thing about bankruptcy is that you know which assets are protected and which are not before you file. In most states, you can often keep your car, home, clothing, jewelry, household items, and 100% of retirement accounts. The property you get to keep after filing for bankruptcy depends on your state's "exemptions". Each state has an exemption law that delineates the type and amount of property a debtor can keep away from his creditors. All states allow you to keep 100% of your retirement accounts. That is why I always preach never to touch your retirement accounts to pay debt. Otherwise, you are sacrificing your financial future for a debt problem that exists today.

States vary between the type and amount of property someone can keep after filing for bankruptcy. The following is a list of exemptions for those who file for Chapter 7 bankruptcy protection in Colorado:

- $1,500 - Wearing apparel ($3,000 if married)
- $1,500 - Personal books, family pictures ($3,000 for married couples)
- $2,000 - Jewelry and watches ($4,000 if married)
- $3,000 - Household goods ($6,000 if married)
- $5,000 - Motor vehicle equity ($10,000 if married) and double that if over 60 or disabled
- $20,000 - Tools of trade, i.e., things you need for your job ($40,000 for married couples)
- $50,000 - Farm machinery, tools, livestock
- $50,000 - Cash surrender value of life insurance, except contributions within 2 years

- $60,000 - Home equity for primary residence ($90,000 if you're over 60)
- 100% - Retirement accounts: IRA, 401(k), 457, 403, pension plan, etc.

Your rights to receive certain benefits, such as social security, unemployment compensation, veteran's benefits, public assistance, and pensions are completely exempt regardless of the amount received. No one can take away those future benefits if you file bankruptcy.

In determining whether property is exempt, you must keep a few things in mind. The value of property is not the amount you paid for it, but what it is worth today. For determining the value of furniture, garage sale prices are the norm. For a car, the National Automobile Dealers Association (NADA) or Kelly Blue Book provide reliable values. Basically, the value of exempt property is based on how much you could sell the asset for at the time you file bankruptcy.

Bankruptcy protects cars and homes depending on the amount of equity held in the property. Equity in property, such as a home, is the value after sales commissions and loans. This means you count your exemptions against the fair market value of property less sale commissions that would be paid and any money you owe on the property. For example, if you own a $300,000 house with a $240,000 mortgage, you would count your exemptions against the $300,000 value, less $21,000 for sales commission (assuming 7%) and less $240,000 for the mortgage owed, which would leave you with $39,000 in equity.

What happens if you are above the exemption amounts or you have unprotected assets? In Chapter 7, the trustee has the right to sell the property and disburse the proceeds to your creditors. Some trustees allow the debtors to buy back the items from the trustee. Assume your car has $1,000 more equity than is allowed under your state law exemption. In that instance, the trustee will let you pay the $1,000 to keep the car. For some assets, it makes sense to "cut a deal" with the trustee because you can buy back your assets and get out of debt for pennies on the dollar.

Another option is to sell unprotected assets before you file for Chapter 7. Many Internet postings advise against selling any property before filing for bankruptcy as it may be seen as keeping an asset out of the hands of a trustee. However, anyone can sell property before filing for bankruptcy so long as the asset is sold at fair market value. Some people advise against selling assets to friends and family members as that may be considered a "preference" sale, but if the asset is sold for fair market value, there is no problem. If you sell your $10,000 Mercedes to your mother for $5, then you have a problem. But if your mother pays you $9,500 for the car, then it is a fair market transaction and legitimate prior to filing bankruptcy.

If you do sell an asset prior to filing for Chapter 7 bankruptcy, and assuming it was at fair market value, the next question you have to answer is, "what did you do with the money?" This is where people get into trouble. Some people will sell the car at fair market value and then give the money to their father to repay a loan from him. That is a preference payment the trustee can recover. Your father would have to return the money to the trustee. Instead, invest the proceeds in a retirement account, pay your taxes, or spend it on personal needs.

Some people fear Chapter 7 because they worry the trustee will sell their home and other assets even though it rarely happens. The latest statistic from the U.S. Trustee Program with the Department of Justice, which is the federal agency that oversees bankruptcy cases and trustees, is that only 5% of Chapter 7 cases have any assets that can be sold. This means 95% of the people who file for Chapter 7 bankruptcy do not lose anything.

Chapter 7 is a powerful way to get out of debt, and with all powerful tools, there are some restrictions. In October 2005, the bankruptcy reform laws were revised with a new requirement: a "means test." This test evaluates your income to determine if you are eligible to have your debts dismissed completely under Chapter 7 or whether you need to enter into a debt restructuring plan under Chapter 13.

You may qualify to file Chapter 7 bankruptcy if your income falls below the median income in your resident state based on your family size. For example, in Colorado, if you are a single person who makes less than $50,000 per year, then you can file for Chapter 7. If you earn more than the median income, you may still qualify for Chapter 7 provided you are unable to set aside at least 25% of your income to repay your creditors. If you don't qualify for Chapter 7, it doesn't mean you cannot file bankruptcy as there are two other bankruptcies available.

Chapter 13

Chapter 13 bankruptcy is an alternative for those who do not qualify to file Chapter. A Chapter 13 allows you spread out the payment of your debts over a 3-5 year period at an amount you can afford in your budget. Chapter 13 may be the right choice if you have valuable property you want to keep and would lose if you filed for Chapter 7. Chapter 13 allows you to keep all of your assets so long as you repay the asset's value to your unsecured creditors. This is true even if you are behind on the payments on your house or car.

One advantage of a Chapter 13 is that it protects joint account holders and co-signers from collection activity. In a Chapter 7 case, creditors can go after co-signers after your bankruptcy discharges your liability. Chapter 13 protects co-signers while you are in the repayment period. It also gives you the option of discharging certain debts that are not discharged in a Chapter 7 bankruptcy filing, such as marital property settlements.

You can file Chapter 13 if your unsecured debts are less than $360,475[11] and the amount you owe on secured debts is less than $1,081,400[12]. You must have sufficient income to pay for your monthly living expenses before entering into a Chapter 13 plan. If you do, Chapter 13 is a good solution because it allows you to repay your debts on a budget you can afford.

The amount you pay in a Chapter 13 bankruptcy to unsecured creditors, such as credit cards, will be based on your disposable income. This is calculated by taking your gross income less payroll deductions minus "legitimate and necessary expenses." These are based on IRS standards for basic living expenses for utilities, rent or mortgage, automobiles, insurance, etc. There is a cap on these expenses and the cap may not bear any relation to your actual expenses. For example, the IRS permits a utility expense of $275 per month. If you spend more than that, you can't count the excess amount as a deduction from your disposable income. Also, not every personal expense can be deducted. For example, if you own a horse and the cost is $250 per month, that expense will not reduce your disposable income.

Typically, Chapter 13 drastically lowers your monthly debt payments because you are paying what you can afford instead of the creditor's minimum payment. The amount you repay varies, but with proper planning there are steps

_____

[11] This number is in the U.S. Code and is based on inflationary increases as of September 2013.
[12] Ibid.

you can take to lower the monthly amount while benefiting your family. Some people who are struggling with debt will cancel their health insurance. In a Chapter 13 though, you are encouraged to maintain health insurance as a "legitimate and necessary expense". Even charitable contributions and supporting elderly parents are encouraged for those repaying debts under Chapter 13.

Chapter 13 has a few "tricks" that I really like. First, Chapter 13 is a way to eliminate a second mortgage. If you own a home that is worth $225,000 with a first mortgage of $250,000 and a second mortgage of $75,000, the second mortgage of $75,000 can be removed. During the last recession, this legal remedy was employed by thousands of homeowners whose homes were "underwater". Before you feel guilty about it, remember, this practice is permissible under federal law. The process only works if the value of your home is worth less than the balance of your first mortgage. If your home is worth $251,000, you would not be able to remove the second mortgage.

The surest way to save a home from foreclosure is to file Chapter 13. It is the only option that will stop a foreclosure and permit you to keep your home. In Chapter 13, you take the missed mortgage payments and repay them over three to five years. If you fell $12,000 behind on your mortgage, you could file for Chapter 13 and repay that money over five years at $200 per month, but you have to resume making your normal mortgage payment as well. Thus, if you don't have the income to make your normal mortgage payment, Chapter 13 won't help you. But if you fell behind on your mortgage because you lost your job and are now employed, then Chapter 13 is a good option to save your home.

Another benefit of Chapter 13 is the ability to refinance cars. Financing cars is generally a poor financial decision because you're paying interest on an asset that depreciates. As a result, you are likely to owe more to the bank than what the car is worth. Chapter 13 allows a debtor to refinance a car to repay what the asset is worth instead of what is owed. Assume you have a car worth $7,500 and owe $14,000. Under Chapter 13, you can pay off the car at $7,500 instead of $14,000. You can also lower your interest rate. I've been able to help my clients reduce interest rates from 24% to 5% under a Chapter 13. That is a huge savings.

Chapter 13 allows you to repay taxes without accruing future interest and penalties. Some taxes are dischargeable, which we'll discuss later, but taxes from the last three years typically need to be repaid. A Chapter 13 is a way to pay your tax debt without incurring future penalties or interest. Again, the savings can be huge.

Finally, under a Chapter 13, you can keep all of your property if your plan meets the requirements of the bankruptcy law. If you exceed the exemptions that we discussed under Chapter 7, then you pay excess amount to unsecured creditors and still keep the property. For example, if you own a car that is over the exemption by $4,500, then you need to pay $4,500 to your unsecured creditors over three to five years. The good news is that this lowers the payment and you get to keep your car.

Chapter 11

Chapter 11 bankruptcy is a way for an individual, partnership, or corporation to file for debt relief and restructure. It works very well if you have an extremely large amount of personal or business debt and a mix of unsecured and secured loans.

If you're an individual, Chapter 11 bankruptcy may be an option for you if you do not meet the requirements of another bankruptcy, such as Chapter 7 or Chapter 13. As an individual, filing Chapter 11 may help you restructure your mortgages, eliminate taxes, and reduce credit card debt. A personal Chapter 11 is complex, and can only be accomplished by hiring an experienced attorney, which can be very expensive.

If you're a business owner, whether the business is a partnership or corporation, Chapter 11 bankruptcy allows for debt restructuring in order to allow your business to continue its normal operations. The idea behind a Chapter 11 bankruptcy is your business could be profitable if your debt were more manageable.

There are no limits on the amount of debt that can be discharged under a Chapter 11 bankruptcy. Many companies use Chapter 11 as a tool to restructure their debt. A Chapter 11 bankruptcy can help to stop foreclosures, terminate leases, and renegotiate contracts. It can also settle judgments in lawsuits. The most effective tool in Chapter 11 is that it allows you to repay a secured loan at the collateral's value instead of the full loan amount, which could save thousands of dollars.

Chapter 11 is very complex and is a book by itself. For the individual debtor, it only makes sense to consider Chapter 11 if you have more than $1 million dollars in debt and restructuring your personal finances would make you solvent again. Otherwise, most people either file for Chapter 7 or 13. That is why I don't go into much detail about Chapter 11 here except to let you know it may be an option if you're struggling with debt.

Bankruptcy Distinctions

Why did I start this chapter by saying bankruptcy is one of the best debt solutions? First, bankruptcy eliminates most debts, such as from credit cards, personal loans, lines of credit, overdrafts, payday loans, collection accounts, judgments, unpaid homeowner's association dues, foreclosure and repossession deficiencies, etc. It is easier to state it this way: bankruptcy eliminates <u>all debts</u> except child support, alimony/maintenance, restitution, and student loans. Credit counseling only works for credit cards. Debt settlement only works if the creditor agrees to your settlement. With bankruptcy, the law forces the discharge of liabilities and the creditor has very few rights to prevent you from getting out of debt.

Bankruptcy is one of the most misunderstood and misrepresented debt relief options. There are so many "urban myths" about bankruptcy that some people fear it. The truth is that bankruptcy provides many powerful solutions no other debt relief options provide. As we discussed earlier, the only way to stop a foreclosure and save your home is to file for Chapter 13. Some attorneys claim they can file lawsuits to stop the foreclosure, which is possible, but only provide a short term solution. It does not guarantee you can keep your home. It just delays the foreclosure. Only Chapter 13 guarantees you can keep your home, provided you can afford the monthly mortgage payments.

The greatest power of bankruptcy that no other form of debt relief can provide is the "automatic stay". Once you file bankruptcy, creditors must immediately stop all collection activity. An automatic stay stops wage garnishments. Creditors cannot legally repossess your property while in bankruptcy. Bankruptcy is the only debt relief option that has this power.

Bankruptcy can discharge personal income tax obligations. Some people think you can never get rid of a government taxes, but Congress has allowed people to use bankruptcy as a way of eliminating old tax debts. To eliminate tax debt, the tax debt must be more than three years old and the return must have been filed at least two years prior to filing bankruptcy. There are some other requirements, but these are the most important ones. Taxes older than three years are relative to the tax year at the time you filed. I am writing this book in 2013, which means that taxes from 2009, 2008, 2007, and older could be eliminated by filing for bankruptcy. Taxes due for 2010, 2011, and 2012 are still within the last three years and cannot be discharged. However, under Chapter 13, you could repay those taxes (2010-2012) without future penalties or interest.

Bankruptcy protects people who are employed. The bankruptcy code explicitly states that someone cannot be terminated from their job for the sole reason of filing bankruptcy. This even applies to people who work at banks and are discharging debt from their own employers.

There are definite downsides to filing for bankruptcy. Your credit score will drop by at least 60 points. Bankruptcy remains on your credit for ten years as opposed to seven years for debts that are not repaid. Some people worry they won't be able to get credit for the next ten years, but it is not true. You can get credit right away, but at a higher cost. Most people can buy a car the day after they file Chapter 7; however, the interest rate will be above 12%. You will get credit card offers, but the limits will be very low – typically less than $1,000 per card. Bankruptcy does not erase a poor banking history. If you have had a history of bad checks and overdrawn accounts, that information remains on your banking record for seven years despite no longer being obligated to pay those debts.

Despite the hit your credit record will take by filing for bankruptcy, it is possible to rebuild your credit. In fact, it typically takes 1-2 years to restore your credit after filing Chapter 7 bankruptcy. It's very possible to have a 720 credit score within one year after filing for bankruptcy, qualify to buy a home with a FHA mortgage, obtain credit cards again, and buy a car at a low interest rate. Whereas it takes seven years to recover after completing credit counseling or debt settlement.

Bankruptcy is a matter of public record. Many people don't like hearing that. Some local newspapers will publish the names of people who file for bankruptcy, but in general, the public at large does not know if you file unless they are search a federal database called PACER. However, whenever you apply for a new loan, that person or company will know you filed for bankruptcy, but the fear of someone knowing about it should never hold you back from getting out of debt.

Not all property can be protected in a bankruptcy. A rental property with equity, a time share, stocks, bonds, and other investment type of assets can be lost if you file Chapter 7 bankruptcy. You can keep these items in a Chapter 13 bankruptcy if you repay the value, but sometimes, the value is more than someone can afford to repay. In those situations, debt settlement is going to be a better option.

Using bankruptcy correctly and strategically requires the assistance of an attorney. A Chapter 7 may sound simple, but there are so many nuances that can mess up your case. The reality though is attorneys cost money. A good Chapter 7 attorney will cost about $2,000-3,000, and a Chapter 13 filing will run around $3,000-5,000. A Chapter 11 is very expensive and starts at $10,000. But compare these costs to the money you'll save and the costs will be negligible.

I always ask my potential clients if I could settle their $50,000 debt for $2,000, would they take that deal? The answer, of course, is "yes" because it's a great offer. The $2,000 you pay the attorney for a Chapter 7 filing will get rid of $50,000 of debt. That's how to think of attorney fees.

One thing most bankruptcy attorneys recommend is you stop paying your credit cards and use the monthly savings to pay your attorney. It's the best way to approach the fee issue, but don't delay. If you wait too long, then creditors might sue you and start garnishing your wages. Once you decide to file for bankruptcy, file as soon as possible.

I like bankruptcy because it is predictable. It is a federal law with several decades of history and case law. When I look at someone's debt situation, I can predict with 99% certainty the outcome of filing bankruptcy. That is powerful and it helps people overcome their fears about getting out of debt.

Bankruptcy is something you can rely upon to get out of debt. Its origins and purpose are to restore trust by giving people the chance to rebuild their financial futures. My bankruptcy clients have confidence they will get out of debt, rebuild their credit, and keep their important possessions. They trust the bankruptcy laws and legal system to help them rebuild their financial lives, and most importantly, they trust me to help them.

> *"I wanted to send a thank you letter to you for your services that you provided me with the Chapter 7 Bankruptcy. It has been over a year since the discharge but as I reflect back on how things unfolded, I can't thank you enough. Not just for getting the bankruptcy done but essentially for talking me through what the best options were and why. One year later I still feel so much more relieved than trying to manage everything myself. Although I am sending you this letter a year after our bankruptcy discharge, I still wanted to send it so that you knew how I felt and how things been progressing for me. Overall, I am once again thankful for how the process went. Thank you."*
>
> *-Joshua N.*

Summary of Bankruptcy Pros and Cons

PROS	CONS
Bankruptcy is a federal law with known legal rules and procedures.	Not everyone can file bankruptcy due to legal restrictions applicable to Chapter 7 and 13.
Bankruptcy solves most debt problems, including foreclosure, credit cards, personal loans, medical bills, payday loans, judgments and repossession deficiencies, etc.	Bankruptcy is complicated and difficult to do without an attorney.
Bankruptcy stops creditors from suing a person and stops any wage garnishments.	Bankruptcy does not help with student loans, child support, or alimony.
You can successfully plan a successful outcome by using an experienced attorney.	Bankruptcy stays on your credit report for 10 years.
Bankruptcy eliminates tax debt older than three years and allows the repayment of newer tax debt without future interest and penalties.	Bankruptcy filings are public record.
Bankruptcy can save a home from foreclosure, remove a second mortgage from a house, and refinance automobiles at a lower monthly payment.	There is a social stigma to bankruptcy.

PROS	CONS
A person can get and rebuild credit within two years of filing bankruptcy.	"Un-Exempt" assets are lost when filing bankruptcy.
You can keep important assets, such as your home, car, personal and household items, and retirement.	

"I'm a client of Kevin Heupel and he really made the situation so much less stressful. Kevin showed me how I would come out of this in a better place – and he was right."

-Christina T.

NOTES

_____

_____

_____

_____

_____

_____

_____

_____

_____

_____

_____

_____

_____

_____

_____

_____

_____

CHAPTER SIX: Loan Modifications

The Great Recession of the 21st Century saw an explosion in foreclosures. Several million people lost their homes as they could not afford their mortgage payments, while other homeowners found the home they owned was worth far less than the outstanding mortgage balance. As a result, people were leaving their homes and letting the banks foreclose on the property. At the height of the foreclosure wave, one-quarter of homeowners were behind on their mortgage payments. Millions of additional homeowners were trapped in adjustable rate mortgages with rates soaring, leaving no option to refinance since their home's value had dropped.

To stem the rising tide of foreclosures, President Barack Obama announced a $75 billion plan that would help up to nine million people keep their homes in a housing market ravaged by foreclosures. The plan was commonly known as HAMP, which stands for the Home Affordable Modification Program.

HAMP, which began in March 2009, is a federal program that allows homeowners to lower their mortgage payment to 31% or less of their gross monthly income. The program suddenly gave hope to homeowners struggling to make mortgage payments or facing foreclosure.

When HAMP first began, struggling homeowners were excited. More than 5.1 million modification arrangements were initiated as of August 2011; this was double the number of foreclosures at the time. HAMP was originally set to expire after a few years, but President Obama extended the program through December 31, 2015.

Under HAMP, a loan modification involves your lender modifying your existing mortgage payment to make it affordable. A HAMP loan modification can change the interest rate, restructure the term of the loan, and remove delinquent fees. HAMP also allows an adjustable rate mortgage to be converted into a fixed interest rate loan.

The primary focus of HAMP is reducing monthly payments to 31% or less of a person's gross monthly income. For example, if your gross monthly income is $5,000 per month, then your mortgage payments should be $1,550 per month or less. If your mortgage consumes a higher percentage of your income, the goal HAMP is to reduce your monthly mortgage payment.

One of my greatest HAMP successes involved a client who had a mortgage payment of $2,695 per month. He was behind on his payments by $12,243. After a loan modification, his new payment dropped to $1,770 per month. This saved him $925 month and the overdue penalties were removed.

To qualify for HAMP, a homeowner must meet the following requirements:

- The homeowner must have obtained the mortgage on or before January 1, 2009;
- He must owe up to $729,750 on the primary residence;

- The property must not have been condemned;

- The homeowner must be experiencing a financial hardship and is either delinquent or in danger of falling behind on his mortgage payments;

- He must have sufficient, documented income to support a modified payment; and

- He must not have been convicted within the last ten years of felony, larceny, theft, fraud or forgery, money laundering or tax evasion, in connection with a mortgage or real estate transaction.

The application to initiate the loan modification process can be found at www.MakingHomeAffordable.gov. Click on "Request a Modification" under the "Get Started" tab.

The application, which you need to print out and complete, consists of three forms and requires income documentation along with prior tax returns. The application is submitted directly to the mortgage company rather than the federal government. Be sure to send it by Certified Mail so you have proof of the submission as many applications get lost by the banks. Ideally, you would expect to receive a response within 60 days; however, in practice it generally takes four to ten months to get an initial response.

HAMP was forced upon the banks by the federal government, and as a result, many were not in a position to handle the large influx of applications while simultaneously pursing thousands of foreclosures. Worse yet, applications were getting lost, and if the process had been going on for several months, the mortgage companies would require updated financial information. The submission process can be very frustrating and is an exercise in patience for many applicants. If a homeowner was hoping to avoid a foreclosure by obtaining a loan modification, in some instances, the loan modification would come too late.

A loan modification is not available to someone who just wants to lower his monthly mortgage payment. The homeowner must show proof of financial hardship that warrants a modification, such as a pending foreclosure, bankruptcy, etc. Once the application is received, the mortgage company will evaluate the homeowner's income, debt, and hardship eligibility criteria.

The best proof of financial hardship is missing mortgage payments as this demonstrates the home may no longer be affordable. Such hardship can be caused by job loss, loan payment increase, decrease in income, divorce, medical expenses, etc.

If your answer to any of the following questions is "Yes," you may qualify for HAMP:

- Are you behind on your mortgage payments?
- Are you upside-down on your mortgage (meaning that you owe more than the house is worth)?
- Are you in an adjustable, option ARM, or negative amortization loan?
- Are you contemplating bankruptcy?

The mortgage company will apply sequential steps known as "The Waterfall" to reduce monthly mortgage payments to 31% of gross (pre-tax) income or less. The first step is to capitalize outstanding interest, escrow advances, and out-of-pocket servicing expense. This is basically a fancy way of removing late fees. The second step involves reducing the interest rate to 2% for five years, and then increase the interest rate by 1% each year with a cap at 5%. The third step is to look at extending the mortgage term up to 40 years. Finally, the mortgage company will defer a portion of principal (charge interest only on a portion of the principal, not the entire amount), interest-free, until the loan is paid off.

The process is fairly simple until it comes to the Net Present Value (NPV) test. The NPV test is a complex, nonlinear mathematical model to analyze cost/benefit of investment decisions. In general, NPV refers to the present value of a cash-generating investment, such as a bond or mortgage loan. When an investor is faced with a choice between two alternative investments – specifically, between the timing and amount of the cash flows for each investment – the investor obviously prefers the choice with the higher present value. If the NPV test is positive on "The Standard Waterfall," the mortgage company must modify the loan. If the NPV test is negative, the mortgage company may modify the loan in accordance with investor guidelines, but typically will reject the HAMP application.

In the case of a mortgage borrower who has become financially distressed, the investor or a third-party loan servicer faces a choice of whether to modify the mortgage or leave it as is. Each choice generates expected cash flows and the present values of these two cash flows are likely to be different. If the loan is modified, there is a greater chance the borrower will eventually be able to repay the loan in full. If not, there is a higher likelihood the loan will go to foreclosure and the investor will absorb the associated losses. If the NPV of the modified loan is higher than the NPV of the loan as is, a modification is said to be "NPV positive."

HAMP is structured to produce modifications that are likely to test NPV positive; thereby, increasing the number of modifications that will be done and keeping more Americans in their homes. It does this, first, by lowering the probability that borrowers will default by making payments more affordable, and second, by providing incentive payments to the banks for successful loan modifications.

The NPV test gives great flexibility to the mortgage companies as they can assign their own risk. As such, some mortgage lenders are reluctant to issue loan modifications. As the values of homes dropped precipitously, it was difficult to generate a positive NPV. As a result, I saw many clients who failed to get a loan modification due to failing the NPV test.

Clients' fortunate enough to satisfy the NPV analysis entered the HAMP trial period. The servicer offers a three-month trial modification (or up to four months if the borrower is in imminent default). The homeowner does not have to sign the trial period plan notice. Instead, he must make a payment each month during the trial period. Missing a single payment results in the trial modification being revoked. After a successful trial period, the homeowner is eligible for permanent modification.

What some homeowners fail to realize is that entering the trial modification period can affect your credit. This is because the trial modification payment is lower than the normal payment; as a result, your payment is considered a late payment because the entire amount was not paid in full. Each month you pay less than your original payment constitutes a late payment entry to your credit report. After three months, you will have a 90-day late notice on your mortgage, which can dramatically reduce your credit score. If you want to keep your home though, you have no alternative.

For a successful trial period to become a permanent modification, the homeowner must return a signed modification agreement to the servicer. Homeowners who make timely payments receive a principal reduction of up to $5,000, which is $1,000 per year for five years based on an interest of 2%. More importantly, the interest rate adjustment allows for a gradual transition to a sustainable payment amount. Increasing by 1% each year after the first five years, but capped at a total increase of 5% in year eight.

Another benefit of HAMP is the Principal Reduction Alternative (PRA). PRA gives loan servicers the flexibility to offer principal reduction relief to homeowners whose homes are worth significantly less than they still owe. To qualify, the (loan-to-value needs to be 115% or above. This means that if the amount owed on the home relative to the value of the home is greater than 115 %, the loan servicer must consider whether to reduce the principal. However, principal reduction is at the servicer's discretion. For further information about Principal Reduction under HAMP, see: http://www.irs.gov/uac/Principal-Reduction-Alternative-Under-the-Home-Affordable-Modification-Program.

HAMP is designed to protect homeowners from unnecessary and costly foreclosure actions. A mortgage company may not refer a homeowner to foreclosure until the homeowner is either determined to be ineligible for HAMP, declines HAMP, or contact efforts have failed. If you are facing foreclosure, contact your mortgage company or call the HAMP Hotline at 888-995-HOPE (4673). Remember though, HAMP is not a guarantee to stop a foreclosure so remember Chapter 13 as an option.

If a homeowner is denied a modification under HAMP, that is not the end of the road. Banks now approve loan modifications in-house. Many of my clients have been more successful with modifying their mortgages directly with the lender than relying on HAMP.

As with any debt solution, there are problems with loan modifications. Some homeowners receive a loan modification they cannot afford and still end up losing the homes to foreclosure. Other modifications result in the homeowner making payments on an "underwater" asset that may take years to recover before there is no equity in the home, which means that the homeowner is wasting a lot of money during that time. And loan modifications only help with mortgage payments. If you have other debts, a loan modification will not resolve them. It might provide some more income you can pay towards other debts, but it does not immediately provide relief from other debts. Regardless of these drawbacks, HAMP is one program that I tell my clients not to fear because they will be no worse off for trying even if the loan modification gets denied. However, they'll certainly be better off if it gets approved. There's nothing to lose by trying.

There are companies and attorneys you can hire to help with the loan modification process. Keep in mind you don't need to pay anyone as the process is fairly simple. There have been a lot of loan modification scams where the firm requires payment before the process begins, and then the firm disappears. The State of California passed a law in October 2009 prohibiting real estate brokers and attorneys from accepting advanced fees for the purpose of a loan modification. Regardless, there are legitimate companies that can help. Instead of wasting your time collecting and submitting documents, sometimes it's worth the expense of hiring a company that can do it more efficiently as the process can easily take 40-60 hours of your time.

Loan modifications are all the rage today. I don't see it being a long-term solution though. If it's an option for you today, then I suggest you take advantage of the opportunity now as there are some great benefits to the program before HAMP expires.

> *"I have been struggling to hold on and not getting anywhere. After meeting Kevin Heupel, I felt a lot of relief and he was able to answer all of my questions."*
>
> *-Nancy D.*

Summary of Loan Modifications Pros and Cons

PROS	CONS
Loan modifications reduce monthly mortgage payments to less than 31% of the homeowner's gross monthly income.	Only available to homeowners who can document a "financial hardship".
Interest rates are lowered to 2% for the first five years and cap at 5%.	The process can take 4-10 months.
A loan modification can convert an adjustable-rate mortgage into a fixed-rate loan.	The federal loan modification program has a future expiration date.
Loan modifications are easy to do and people can submit a loan modification without hiring an attorney.	Loan modifications do not stop foreclosure sales.
	A loan modification is not a legal right or a guarantee; the bank makes the decision based on what's best for the bank.
	Does not get rid of negative equity in a home.

NOTES

CHAPTER SEVEN: Offers in Compromise

According to Tom Abrahams, a reporter for KTRK in Houston, about 8.2 million Americans owed more than $83 billion in back taxes, penalties and interest as of June 22, 2009. That's more than $10,000 per person. That same year, the IRS had 3.8 million tax delinquency investigations. It added 2.5 million new ones, closed another 2.7 million, which still left it with 3.7 million tax returns to investigate.

Taxes are like any other debt. When money gets tight or times get tough, it becomes difficult to pay your taxes when doing so competes with your ability to pay for food and shelter. What people fail to realize is that there are settlement options available for taxes. Some people think taxes never go away. As I discussed earlier in this book, bankruptcy allows a taxpayer to eliminate taxes that are more than three years old. However, bankruptcy may not be a good option for someone whose only debt is taxes so it's important to consider other solutions.

The most popular solution for resolving a tax burdens is called an "offer in compromise." The IRS recognizes that some people do not have the ability to pay their outstanding tax debts, and thus need some relief. An offer in compromise allows you to settle your tax debt for less than the full amount owed.

In considering an offer in compromise, the IRS considers your unique set of facts and circumstances, including:

- Ability to pay;
- Income;
- Expenses; and
- Asset equity.

The IRS generally approves an offer in compromise when the amount offered represents the most the IRS can expect to collect within a reasonable period of time. However, what is "reasonable" to the IRS may not seem reasonable to you.

There are strict requirements to qualify for an offer in compromise. First, you must have filed all tax returns, made all required estimated tax payments for the current year, and if you are a business owner, made all required federal tax deposits for the current quarter. You cannot be in an open bankruptcy proceeding while seeking an offer in compromise, nor be disputing part or all of the tax debt owed. To submit an offer in compromise, you must pay a $150 filing fee and submit a simple application to the IRS. The application is a personal financial statement so the IRS can determine whether a reduction in tax liability is warranted.

There are two requirements that lead to a successful offer in compromise. The first is that your monthly disposable income needs to be very low. The IRS uses its own standard with predetermined regional allowances for basic needs such as utilities, food, clothing, transportation, etc. These numbers are pretty stringent, and many Americans would find it difficult to live on an IRS budget. For example, the IRS allows $240 per month for transportation expense, which includes expenses related to gas, taxes, insurance, and other related vehicle expenses. Given the current price of gas, $240 is not much and certainly doesn't take into consideration the varying tax rates among different municipalities. The second factor is you have no assets. This means that you can have no cash in the bank, no equity in your house, no retirement funds, etc. The IRS expects people to sell their homes if they have equity in order to pay their taxes, unlike bankruptcy that allows you to keep your home. The end result is that an offer in compromise will have little success if you have assets but no money to pay the tax.

The most obvious benefit of an offer in compromise is the process has the potential to substantially reduce your tax liability to a level consistent with your ability to pay. An offer in compromise will put the collection activities of other creditors on hold unless your salary or bank account is currently being garnished. If you have an approved installment agreement with IRS and are making installment payments, then you may stop making those installment payments when you submit the offer. If your offer is rejected for any reason, your installment agreement with IRS will be reinstated with no additional fee. Another benefit is that tax liens are be relinquished by the IRS within 30 days of receiving the agreed amount from an offer in compromise, which immediately boosts your credit rating.

As with all good things, there are some drawbacks. Penalties and interest, which currently amount to 12% per year, continue to accrue during the offer evaluation process. Also, the settlement must be paid within 24 months, which can be difficult depending upon your income and tax debt. Once an offer is agreed to and accepted, you are obligated to file upcoming tax returns and make tax payments on time for the next five years. This applies to payroll tax and estimated business taxes in addition to income taxes. All tax refunds owed to you before your offer is accepted, and during the year of acceptance by the IRS, must be forfeited and go toward paying your existing IRS debt. You may also have to forfeit refunds for the next three to five years. After submitting an offer in compromise, you may not appeal any outstanding judgments to the IRS or tax court for the number of years stated in the offer. This applies whether the offer is accepted or rejected.

The IRS will revoke an offer in compromise after acceptance if you were untruthful, so never lie about your income or assets. If the offer is revoked, you will be liable for the entire initial amount plus all penalties and interest that accrued during the time the offer was being evaluated.

When considering all this, keep in mind you can only weigh the pros and cons of an offer in compromise in the context of the other options available to you. One thing to remember is that the IRS cannot collect taxes from you forever. The Collection Statute Expiration Date (CSED) prevents the IRS from collecting taxes after ten years from the filing date of the tax return. While that might sound like great news for some people, the IRS consideration of an offer in compromise, which can take up to a year to process, "tolls" the CSED, basically freezing it in place while your submission is reviewed. This means the ten-year clock that normally would allow your tax debt to expire stops ticking. This may not be good if you are close to the end of that time period. If you are, then it's probably best to let the time expire before submitting an offer in compromise.

Another option is to seek non-collectible status. You do this by submitting Form 433-F to an IRS Revenue Officer or the IRS Automated Collection System unit. This takes you out of the collections process without fear of levy or garnishment and you do not have to pay down your liability while in non-collection status. However, a federal tax lien may be filed against you at any time, most likely the instant you have enough money to satisfy the original tax obligation, and frequent reviews of your uncollectible status might result in your removal at any time. Non-collectible status does not resolve the problem, but it might provide enough time to enter into an installment agreement with the IRS at a future date.

The final two options to consider are penalty abatement and innocent-spouse relief. A request for penalty abatement can partially relieve a taxpayer's liability for reasons such as IRS error or delay, erroneous written advice by the IRS, or reasonable cause.

Innocent-spouse relief is a method for one spouse on a joint return who is assessed additional taxes based on the erroneous filing by the other spouse to avoid the penalty. There are several requirements, but generally the "innocent" spouse must not have known of the understated income by the other spouse, and thus, making it unfair to hold the innocent spouse responsible.

A person can file an offer in compromise by himself. The forms required are quite simple and the IRS does a good job of describing the process on their Web site: www.IRS.gov. Before submitting an offer in compromise, I recommend consulting a tax attorney who can provide advice as to whether it makes sense to purse an offer in compromise. There are a lot of companies that advertise tax relief, but be careful as many do not employ tax attorneys on their staff. Also, the fees can be exorbitant given the small amount of work required to submit an offer in compromise.

Summary of Offer in Compromise Pros and Cons

PROS	CONS
You can settle the tax debt for less than you owe.	Taxpayer must remain current with all future tax liabilities and requirements.
An offer in compromise does not require a lot of paperwork.	An offer in compromise is very limited as to who can qualify.
A person can execute an offer in compromise without an attorney.	Bankruptcy or "non-collectible status" can be a better alternative.
An offer in compromise stops any collection efforts by the IRS.	Failure to complete the offer in compromise results in revocation of the agreement and the taxpayer is liable for the initial amount plus all the penalties and interest.
An offer will relinquish any outstanding tax liens.	

> "I first saw Kevin Heupel on the TV Show 'Colorado & Co.' He made me feel the firm could really help me through my disturbing times. Everyone I dealt with at this law firm has been pleasant and very knowledgeable and helpful. I will recommend Heupel Law to anyone. I have complete confidence in the entire team and I thank you so much for all your help and courtesy to me.
>
> "
>
> -Robert H.

NOTES

_____

_____

_____

_____

_____

_____

_____

_____

_____

_____

_____

_____

_____

_____

_____

_____

CHAPTER EIGHT: Student Loans

The price of education has become so expensive that many students need to borrow money to go to college. Upon graduating, some students find they cannot afford to repay their student loans.

According to the College Board Advocacy and Policy Center ("the Center"), by September 30, 2011, 9.1% of borrowers who had entered the repayment process in 2009-10 had defaulted on their federal student loans. This was the highest default rate since 1996. The Center further discovered that students who had left school without completing their degree or certificate were significantly more likely than those who had completed their programs to default on their loans. The Center further estimated the total cost of default for loans issued in 2012-13 will be about $38 billion.

Repaying student loans can be very stressful, especially if the payments are too high. Many people think there is nothing they can do about their student loans; however, there are options. These solutions apply both to private student loans and federal student loans. Some people are able to lower their outstanding balances, and most people are eligible to reduce their monthly payments to one they can afford. People who work for non-profit or government agencies can eliminate their student loans just after ten years.

The following is a list of the most common options available for someone with student loans:

- Consolidation
- Rehabilitation
- Forgiveness-Cancellation
- Deferment/Forbearance
- Standard Repayment
- Graduated Repayment
- Extended Repayment
- Income-Based Repayment
- Income-Contingent Repayment
- Income-Sensitive Repayment
- Pay as You Earn Repayment

The best solution will always depend on the type of loan, a person's income, payment history, and amount owed. The hardest part of repaying student loans is that interest accrues during the life of the loan, even during periods of nonpayment. If someone does not take action towards repaying his student loans, he can find that the outstanding balance will double from the original amount borrowed. Like any other debt, burying your head in the sand is not the right option for handling student loans.

The first consideration before repaying student loans is whether the borrower is entitled to a discharge. The word "discharge" means the same under student loans as it does in the context of bankruptcy, which is you don't have to repay the debt.

There are several options for getting a discharge. The most popular and common discharge option is upon "total and permanent disability" of the borrower. The standard is very similar to someone receiving social security disability income (SSDI). If you receive SSDI and have student loans, you should seek a discharge of your student loan debt as you will not have the income to repay the outstanding loans.

Student loans can also be discharged for school-related issues. For example, if a borrower went to a school that closed within 90 days of enrollment or withdrew from the school, then the borrower can petition the Department of Higher Education for a discharge. A student can also discharge a student loan if the school issued a false certification reflecting the borrower's ability to apply for a student loan. For example, if the school falsely claimed the borrower is a high school graduate when in fact the borrower is not, then the borrower can discharge the student loan. The same applies if the school forges or alters the loan note or engages in identity theft.

There is student loan assistance for those who end up in default. For student loans, default is when you have not paid a private student loan for 90 days or a public student loan for 9 months. Default is a serious and costly situation as there is a 25% collection penalty on borrowers who default on student loans. The worst thing about default is that 15% of your disposable income can be garnished without any notice pursuant to the Debt Collection

Improvement Act of 1996. The federal government can even intercept a tax refund and offset social security. Other consequences include being ineligible for federal employment and enrolling in Medicare. The best thing to do is to avoid default, but if it happens, there are solutions.

One way to cure a default is to settle the student loans; similar to our earlier discussion about debt settlement. Private student loans can be settled for 30-80 cents on the dollar. Public student loans are more restrictive. You can settle a public student loan by paying 100% of current principal and interest; 100% principal and 50% interest; or 90% principal and 100% interest with no collection fees. For example, if you have a government student loan with $50,000 of principal, $10,000 interest, and $15,000 in collection fees; under option one, the borrower would settle for $60,000 ($50,000 principal plus $10,000 interest). The second option allows the borrower to settle for $55,000 ($50,000 principal plus half of the $10,000 interest). The third option permits settlement at $54,000 (90% of $60,000). The savings are not great, and anyone who could afford to settle student loans at this amount would not be in default.

A better way to cure default is through consolidation. Consolidation involves refinancing any and all of your public student loans directly with the Department of Education. An 18.5% collection fee is applied, but the repayment options can be extended over a period up to 25 years. However, most loans require repayment within ten years. The process takes about 30-90 days, which is a quick solution to cure the default. A borrower can only cure a default through consolidation once. If a borrower has already consolidated his student loans and is in default a second time, then the borrower needs to look at rehabilitation in order to cure the current default.

Rehabilitation is a great way to cure a default on a public student loan. Rehabilitation allows the borrower to make nine consecutive monthly payments at a reasonable and affordable payment; it's a budget-based payment the borrower can afford. The 18.5% collection fee still applies, but the default notation on a credit report will be removed upon successful completion of the rehabilitation program. Similar to consolidation, a borrower can only cure a default by rehabilitation only once.

A default cannot be cured while the loan is still in default. Sometimes the Department of Justice will sue student loan borrowers who are in default and obtain a judgment against them. The judgment must be vacated before a borrower can use rehabilitation or consolidation as a way to cure a default. Judgments can usually be vacated after 34-48 payments at the discretion of the creditor.

There are several payment options available to all student loan borrowers. The basic repayment option is the ten year "standard" repayment plan where you can repay a student loan no sooner than five years and no later than ten years after graduation.

There is a "graduated" repayment plan where the loan is paid off in ten years with an increase in payments every two years. The payments start off lower and increase every two years under the assumption that the borrower is receiving pay raises to support the stepped-up payments.

The next plan is the "extended" repayment where loans more than $30,000 can be repaid over a longer period up to 25 years.

A final option is the "extended graduated" repayment plan where the length of the loan is extended up to 25 years and monthly payments increase every two years. The chart below details the payment consequences of each plan:

Original Student Loan Balance

Monthly Payment Option:	$25K	$50K	$75K	$100,000	$150,000	$200,000
Standard	$246	$492	$738	$984	$1,476	$1,969
Extended	N/A	$248	$371	$495	$743	$991
Extended Graduated	N/A	$142	$213	$283	$425	$567
Graduated	$159	$318	$477	$636	$954	$1,272

Figures obtained from using the student loan calculators found at http://studentaid.ed.gov/repay-loans/understand/plans/income-based/calculator with an assumed interest rate of 3.4%

With all of the above payment plans, the minimum payment must be at least $50 and cover the interest portion of the payment. A borrower can sometimes extend the repayment period to 30 years, but needs to show exceptional circumstances. A borrower can change plans once a year, which allows some flexibility as the borrower's income and job status change over time. The above plans work well if your student loan is a small dollar amount relative to your income; i.e., less than 20% of your gross income. Otherwise, the payments will be too expensive. For borrowers who have a lot of student loans and a lower income, there are some income-contingent repayment plans that work better.

The first type of an income-contingent repayment plan is "income based repayment," better known as IBR. A borrower can qualify for IBR if the IBR payment is less than the ten-year standard repayment. IBR considers your family size, income, and loan amount when determining a monthly repayment amount. The following chart shows the monthly IBR repayment based on family size and household income:

Total Household Income

Family Size	$25K	$50K	$75,000	$100,000	$150,000	$200,000
1	$50	$420	$730	$1,050	$1,670	$2,300
2	$0	$350	$660	$970	$1,600	$2,220
3	$0	$280	$590	$900	$1,530	$2,150
4	$0	$210	$520	$830	$1,460	$2,080

Figures from studentaid.ed.gov/repay-loans/understand/plans/income-based/calculator

The monthly payments vary drastically from the earlier chart because the focus is on disposable income and family size rather than the loan balance being paid in full over a specific amount of time.

An important benefit of IBR is that the balance is written off after 20 years for loans taken out on or after 2012. There is no such forgiveness with the other repayment options. If the borrower is a government employee or works for a non-profit organization, the borrower can receive forgiveness of the outstanding balance after ten years. For any school teacher who is buried in student loans, this is an excellent solution.

Another option similar to IBR is "Pay As You Earn" or PAYE. PAYE lowers the IBR calculation from 15% to 10% of disposable income. It also decreases the time for forgiveness from 25 to 20 years. PAYE applies to borrowers who have no loan balance prior to October 2008 and originated a new loan after October 2011.

Unfortunately, the repayment options for public student loans do not apply to private student loans and there are fewer options for remedying those loans. With private student loans, you either need to make the monthly payments or let the loans go into default so you can settle the loan for pennies on the dollar.

A private student loan will usually be assigned to a debt collector after the borrower is 90-120 days late on his payments. There is no ability to cure the default once the student loan is "charged off," which typically occurs when the borrower is 150-180 days late. Unlike a public student loan that can garnish wages without a judgment, a private lender must obtain a judgment against the borrower before wages and bank accounts can be garnished. The post-judgment remedies are based on individual state's laws. There are some states, such as Texas and North Carolina, which do not allow wage garnishments; however, other states, including Colorado, allow up to 25% of wages to be garnished for six months.

Every state has a statute of limitations as to when a lawsuit must be filed, and if it is not filed within that timeframe, the lawsuit can never be filed. In Colorado, there is a six year statute of limitation. This means that if a borrower defaults on a private student loan, the debt collector must file a lawsuit within six years of the "charge off" or the debt collector loses the right to collect the debt.

Student loans are certainly the next debt crises for the United States. However, an educated borrower can take advantage of the government programs and save thousands of dollars. I have an attorney in my office who had $140,000 of law school debt. Her payments were $950 per month. Using IBR, she was able to reduce her monthly payments to $325. That's an annual savings of $7,500!

If you have student loans, regardless if you're struggling to pay your bills, it's worth the time to look at the various student loan repayment options available as you could save thousands of dollars.

Summary of Student Loan Repayment Pros and Cons

PROS	CONS
Several repayment options available for student loans.	Income-based repayment plans are not available to borrowers who are in default.
Public student loans can use income-based repayment plans.	Private student loans have limited repayment options and no income-based programs.
Debt settlement is an option for private student loans.	Understanding all the repayment options can be overwhelming.
Student loan forgiveness available after 10-25 years.	Deferment and forbearance capitalizes interest and increases the loan's balance.
A borrower can cure a default either by consolidation or rehabilitation.	Default can only be cured once with consolidation.

NOTES

_____

_____

_____

_____

_____

_____

CHAPTER NINE: Restoring Credit

Getting out of debt is half the battle. The second part is restoring your credit rating. Unfortunately, debt problems have a negative impact on credit scores. Some financial commentators talk about being your own bank and tell you not to worry about rebuilding credit. However, given the cost of homes and cars these days, this is not realistic. You have to rebuild your credit score.

A credit score is determined by using a mathematical formula that predicts the likelihood of a borrower being able to pay his bills on time and in full. It's known as the FICO score (FICO = Fair Isaac Corporation), and it is the standard credit scoring system used by the three primary credit bureaus: Equifax, TransUnion, and Experian.

Credit scores are used to determine whether you will get credit, and if so, at what interest rate. People with a credit score of 720 and above are considered an excellent risk based on the expectation that they will make their payments in full and on time. As a result, these people get the lowest interest rates when buying a house or car. They can also qualify for credit cards offering the lowest interest rates. As your score drops, however, it becomes harder to get credit. If you do, it will be at a higher interest rate that reflects the lender's risk assessment that you may not be able to repay the debt. It is possible for your credit score to drop below 600 and no one will lend you money unless you have a cosigner with good credit.

FICO uses twenty two criteria to determine a credit score. These criteria including the following factors:

1. Account payment information on all credit accounts.

2. Presence or lack of adverse public records; such as bankruptcy, tax liens, judgments, and collection items.

3. Duration of past due accounts over 90 days.

4. Amount past due.

5. Recent past due accounts and adverse public records.

6. Number of delinquent items.

7. Number of accounts in good standing.

8. Amount owed on all accounts.

9. Amount owed on individual accounts.

10. Type of balance carried.

11. Number of accounts with balances.

12. Utilization rate on revolving accounts.

13. Proportion of balance related to the original amount on installment loans.

14. Average times since accounts were opened.

15. Time since each account was opened.

16. Time since the last account activity.

17. Number of recently opened accounts.

18. Number of credit inquiries.

19. Times since the most recent accounts were opened.

20. Time since the credit inquiries.

21. The re-establishment of positive credit.

22. The mix of various types of credit.

This is an exhaustive list, but the good news is that you do not need to understand each and every item. The bulk of one's credit score comes down to five main items: payment history, outstanding balances, account age, credit type, and inquiries. The following chart shows the importance of each item:

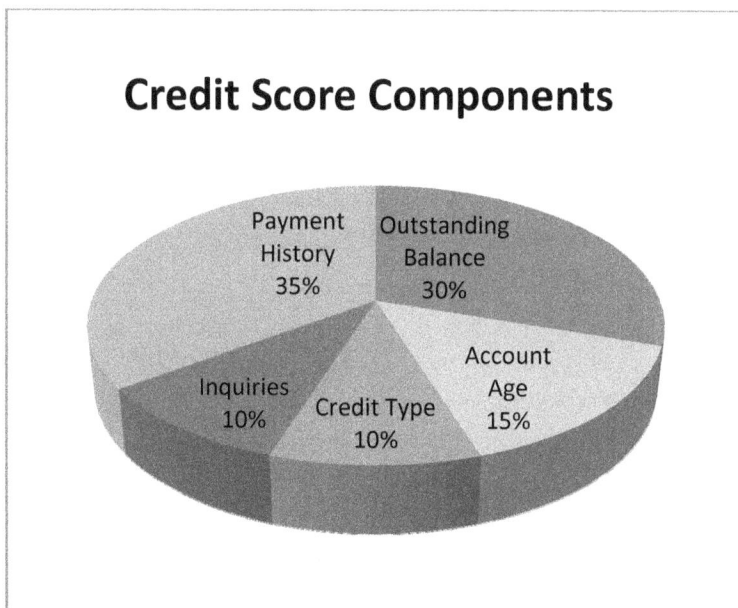

Credit Score Components

Payment History 35%

Outstanding Balance 30%

Account Age 15%

Credit Type 10%

Inquiries 10%

http://www.creditcards.com/credit-card-news/help/5-parts-components-fico-credit-score-6000.php

In order to rebuild credit, it's important to understand some credit myths. Some of these are counterintuitive. For example, some people think if they close their older credit cards, it will help their credit score. That's incorrect. Older accounts improve your score while closing them has a negative impact.

Another myth is that having little credit will help your credit score. This is also not correct. While having little credit will help you avoid financial problems, it doesn't help build a credit score over 700. The reality is that you need to have credit in order to show you can handle credit responsibly. If you can, then your score increases. If not, then your score decreases.

The next popular myth is that you need to maintain a balance on your accounts in order to have a high credit score. This is another belief that can hurt you as you are paying unnecessary interest on credit. It's fine to pay off the account in full each month because the credit bureaus rely on creditors to update the payment history as being paid on time or late, but not the amount of the payment.

Avoiding these popular myths is one way to rebuild your credit history. The next step is understanding the factors that help or hurt your credit score.

Your payment history makes up about 35% of your total score. To have a good payment history, you simply need to make your payments on time for the minimum amount each month. Some people think they can pay their mortgage within 30 days after the due date and still be considered paying on time. That strategy can work if you are only one payment behind as most mortgage companies don't report late payments until you miss 2-3 months of payments. However, it's not worth the risk as payments can easily slip from one month into the next.

The second largest component of your credit score is the amount you owe; this makes up about 30% of your total score. This is based on your "utilization rate", or the amount of debt you carry as a percentage of your credit limits on revolving accounts. Ideally, you want to keep your balance on revolving accounts to less than 30% of the total credit limit. This means if you have a credit card with a limit of $10,000, you never want to carry or show a balance greater than $3,000. Going above 50% of the limit will negatively impact your score; whereas, remaining below 30% shows responsible use of credit.

As mentioned earlier, the length of time you've had credit helps your score. Don't close old accounts, and if you have more than three revolving accounts, then don't open any new accounts.   A person only needs three revolving accounts to build credit. Revolving accounts are credit cards and they can be unsecured or secured as discussed below.

For someone coming out of bankruptcy, getting a credit card can be a frightening proposition. If you want to rebuild your credit, it's a necessity. Credit bureaus give more points when you use credit cards in a responsible manner than if you don't use them at all, as this gives them no way to evaluate your ability to repay a debt. With credit cards, you simply need to keep the balance below

30% of your credit limit and make your minimum monthly payment on time.

Carrying revolving credit rebuilds your credit score more quickly than an installment loan, such as a car loan or mortgage. This is why mortgage and car loan payments have set due dates and stated monthly payments. There is no discretion by the debtor to pay less than the amount owed as the creditor has set the terms. You are not showing the creditor how you can responsibly use credit. With credit cards, you decide what you are going to buy, how much of a balance you are going to pay off or carry each month, when you are going to make your payments, and how much you will pay. This shows more responsibility on your part, and thus, you get higher marks for using revolving credit lines.

Most credit repair experts, such as Philip X. Tirone, author of 7 Steps To a 720 Credit Score, recommend carrying three revolving credit lines. You don't need more than three, and fewer than three doesn't show enough discretion on your part. Three is considered the magic number as it assures lenders you will not abuse your credit privileges. Sometimes it can be hard to get three revolving lines of unsecured credit, especially if you have filed for bankruptcy. If you are having difficulty obtaining credit, you have a couple of options.

The first option is get a secured credit card. A secured credit card is where you put money in the bank and you get a credit card tied to that account. For example, if you put a $1,000 in an account, the bank will give you a secured credit card with a limit of $1,000. As stated above, do not exceed the 30% limit even though you have money in the bank.

The second option is to have someone add you as an authorized user on an existing account. It sounds odd, but by becoming an authorized user, you benefit as you are borrowing another person's past credit history. Be sure this person has good credit or your credit could suffer instead of improve. The person with the credit needs to keep the balance under 30% of the limit and make timely payments. If they are doing that, then becoming an authorized user will increase your credit score.

The last comment about revolving credit is to avoid department store cards. You want to focus on the four major credit cards: Visa, MasterCard, American Express, and Discover. Department store cards don't help with rebuilding credit because the purchasing power is limited to only their store. You can use the major credit cards around the world for a variety of purchases, and thus, it shows more responsible behavior on your part.

Although having three lines of revolving credit is the best way to rebuild your credit history, you should still have at least one installment loan on your credit report as credit bureaus want to see a mix of credit types. The most common items that are purchased with installment loans are cars, boats, furniture, and homes. A car lease is an installment loan as well.

Be sure to avoid installment loans that delay payments for more than 30 days as these types of loans suggest you cannot afford to immediately make the payments. You see these types of loans for furniture stores that advertise "no payments for two years". Be sure to only accept installment loans you can afford within your monthly budget. It doesn't make sense to have a large car payment as it will only add to your financial stress. Also, if your credit score is already above 700, then adding an installment loan is not necessary.

Avoid having too many credit inquiries while restoring your credit. Too many inquiries in a one-year period hurt your score. Requesting your credit report doesn't count as an inquiry or affect your score. Although such inquiries are necessary when buying a home or car, try to have all of your credit inquiries pulled within a 30-day period. The credit bureaus understand that it's common to have several inquiries when shopping for a car so shorten the time span when you are looking for a home or car.

The final issue with credit reporting is accuracy. Creditors and credit bureaus make mistakes. You want to verify the accuracy of your credit limits and reported information. This does not mean removing negative items, such as bankruptcy, if the event actually occurred. I know some of my clients have tried to remove their bankruptcy from their credit reports because they think it hurts their score. While bankruptcy initially reduces your credit score, you can start to rebuild once you take affirmative steps toward restoration. More importantly, if you did file for bankruptcy, then it is appropriate to have the bankruptcy reported on your credit report as it helps. However, if you didn't file, then you must petition to have it removed.

There are several types of mistakes that can appear on one's credit report. There can be duplicate items, incorrect personal information, mistakes about your account information, and items that do not belong on your report. When you find an error, submit a dispute to the credit bureaus showing the error along with documentation to prove the error. The dispute can be submitted via each credit agency's Web site at:

TransUnion: www.TransUnion.com

Equifax: www.Equifax.com

Experian: www.Experian.com

Upon receiving your dispute letter, the agency will begin its investigation by contacting the creditor. The creditor is required to verify the accuracy of item in question. Expect a written response within 30 days. If you don't receive a response, send another dispute letter. Once the item is removed, your credit score will increase.

Although there is a lot more information about credit repair and restoration, I find it is best to focus on the five primary areas that affect your score. The most important thing is to be vigilant and look at your credit score every six months. Some of the major credit cards offer credit score monitoring and their services are very good. The costs range between $5-$15 and are worth the expense if the service provides feedback on how to improve your score.

One final thought about using credit; avoid using credit cards for emergencies. Using a credit card to cover an emergency runs the risk of exceeding the 30% balance limit and can cause financial hardship when trying to make future payments. Dave Ramsey recommends maintaining a $1,000 emergency savings account, an amount typically sufficient to cover the cost of repairing or replacing a household item such as a washer, dryer, TV, or refrigerator. Avoiding using credit for financial emergencies will keep you in good standing and financially sound.

"Kevin Heupel gave me piece of mind. Kevin helped me through bad times and to start over. Thank you."

- Deborah V.

Summary of Rebuilding Credit Pros and Cons

PROS	CONS
Rebuilding credit is not necessary for purchasing a home.	Restoring credit requires action on your part.
Keep credit card balances under 30% of limit.	Interest rates and annual fees are higher when rebuilding credit.
Need three unsecured lines and one installment loan to rebuild credit.	Obtaining credit can be difficult after bankruptcy and debt settlement.
Ensure credit report is accurate at all times.	More than 3 credit inquiries per year can drop your score.
Pay all debts on time.	

NOTES

_____

_____

_____

_____

_____

_____

_____

_____

_____

_____

_____

_____

_____

_____

_____

CHAPTER TEN: Final Thoughts

There are many options when it comes to solving debt problems. The solutions depend on the person's income, assets, and types of debts. There is no "one-size-fits-all" when it comes to getting out of debt.

When dealing with large amounts of debt, it is common for one's emotions to take over and cause confusion, doubt, and fear. Unfortunately, the Internet promotes a lot of incorrect information when it comes to solving debt problems. There are many companies that offer one solution, and in order to sell it, they will make all other solutions sound terrible. Debt settlement companies love to make bankruptcy sound like an awful solution because they lose a client when someone files for bankruptcy. My experience has shown that bankruptcy is the best solution for eight out of ten people dealing with debt because they have waited too long before seeking help. The sooner you seek help, the more options there will be for getting out of debt.

If you are struggling with debt, I recommend you speak with a debt relief attorney who is knowledgeable about credit counseling, debt settlement, bankruptcy, loan modifications, offers in compromise, and student loan repayment options. That way, you get advice on all solutions and will understand the pros and cons as they apply to your unique situation. The best thing about meeting with an attorney is that he can help you get over the stigma you might be feeling about your situation.

In my firm, we look for the right solution for our clients. We know that bankruptcy does not solve all problems and another solution might be required. Sometimes we employ two or three different strategies to solve a client's problem. Regardless of the strategy, we know it will work, and that makes our clients happy. Once a strategy is in place, you will overcome the emotions tied to debt and be able to move forward with your life.

The best way to overcome the emotional hurdles of dealing with overwhelming debt is by seeking answers and finding a solution. Many attorneys offer free consultations so take advantage of those offers. Talk to attorneys who handle a large number of cases. My firm has handled thousands of cases, which means it's likely I've seen and handled debt problems similar to yours in the past. The greatest joy of my work is helping a client see a solution to his debt problem so he can live his life without fear. It's truly a blessing, and if you are struggling with debt, then call someone who can find the right solution for you.

The financial roller coaster of debt can be exhausting and mentally challenging. When you step off the financial roller coaster and overcome the six emotional hurdles preventing you from dealing with your debt problem, you can live a brand new life. In the bankruptcy world, we call it a "Fresh Start." Everyone is entitled to recover from mistakes or unforeseen circumstances that lead to overwhelming debt. There is no shame in asking for help. The only shame is in not doing anything.

To solve your problem, take action today and get help. Please call my office at (720) 443-4030. Life is too short not to enjoy it!

> *Kevin Heupel has made my experience much more pleasant than I expected. Filing for bankruptcy is a difficult choice to make, but the people at Heupel Law have made the decision easier and reassuring. I believe that I am awfully young to be in this situation, but I was never treated differently by anyone at Heupel Law. Being able to make monthly payments on my fees has made my experience even easier. Thank you so much for working with me. I would recommend Heupel Law to anyone in my situation."*
>
> *-Wesley B.*

Glossary

Asset:
Any item that has value that can be converted into cash if it is sold to satisfy a debt.

Bankruptcy:
A federal law (since 1890) that gives every American the right to get out of debt by discharging his obligations.

Charge Off:
When a consumer stops making payments on a credit card debt, the entity to which the money is owed may write-off the debt on its financial statement and sell the debt to a collection agency. They also report the unpaid debt to the credit agencies that evaluate a consumer's creditworthiness. It is still a valid debt that needs to be paid despite the "charge off".

Collection agencies:
Businesses that collects payment of unpaid debts. Collection agencies either "buy" debts from companies that have not been able to collect them, and get to keep what they recover from a consumer, or they work for different businesses and get to keep a portion of what they recover from a consumer.

Credit Counseling:
Conducted through a non-profit organization, credit counseling involves combining all credit card debt and negotiating a lower

interest rate so that the consumer can repay the entire balance of the credit card debt over a five year-period. Results in lower interest but higher monthly payments due to accelerated payment schedule.

Creditor:	The person or entity from whom the debtor has borrowed the money, i.e., the bank, mortgage company, credit card issuer, etc.
Credit Report:	A record of an individual's borrowing, and his or her record of repayment or non-payment. Companies holding credit cards on which payments are not received report non-payment on one's Credit Report, which affects one's Credit Score.
Credit Score:	A numerical assessment of a consumer's ability to pay back a debt based on information in his or her credit record.
Debt:	Money owed in repayment of a loan that is expected to be repaid. The loan may have come in the form of purchases made on a credit card, student loan, medical bill, etc.
Debt Mgmt. Plan:	Under credit counseling, the process of repaying one's credit card debt by making a single payment at a lower interest rate than previously paid.

Debtor:	The person who owes the debt, i.e., you.
Debt Settlement:	After defaulting on a debt, a consumer's debt may be sold to a collection agency, after which the consumer can pay a portion of what is owed, typically 20-50% of the original balance, in a lump sum.
Default:	Failure to pay back a loan by missing a minimum payment on a certain due date.
Foreclosure:	The process of seizing a secured asset (e.g., a home) and selling it in order to collect what is owed for non-payment on the mortgage.
Interest rate:	A percentage fee charged for borrowing money for mortgages, car loans, and credit cards.
Installment credit:	Loans that require a fixed repayment amount on a certain due date, such as a car or home loan (five year car loan or thirty year-mortgage, for example).
Lien:	A legal obligation to repay a debt that is secured by an asset, such as a home or car.
Loan Modification:	Conducted through a federal program known as HAMP (Home Affordable Modification Program), the process involves a homeowner asking his mortgage company to

	reduce his payments to less than 31% of his gross monthly income.
Minimum payment:	The minimum amount that a consumer is expected to pay every month when he or she cannot pay the total balance due. The amount that remains unpaid is generally subject to a high interest rate. Paying only the minimum balance due is a typical way of accumulating debt without realizing it.
Mortgage:	A loan to purchase a home that is secured by the property. If a consumer defaults on too many mortgage payments, the property may be foreclosed upon and seized to pay the overdue amount.
Offer in Compromise:	A formal process with the IRS which allows taxpayers to settle their outstanding tax debts for pennies on the dollar if the debtor is insolvent.
Overdraft:	Banks will often offer consumers an opportunity to have their bills paid at a higher than usual rate of interest up to a limit that is covered by an overdraft account.
Recession:	A slowdown in economic activity which usually involves higher unemployment and the banks not extending credit to people.

Revolving credit:	Credit that is extended without a specific number of payments required to pay it back. Credit cards are examples of revolving credit.
Secured Debt:	Something secured by collateral, such as a car loan or mortgage and if you fail to make the payments, you lose the collateral.
Student loan:	Unsecured loan for the purpose of paying college or graduate school tuition and living expenses. Loans may come from private sources, such as banks, or public sources, such as the federal government.
Unsecured debt:	Debt that is not tied to a tangible asset, like collateral. Refers to credit cards, medical bills, payday loans, lines of credit, personal loans, student loans, taxes, etc.
Trade account:	Types of debt that do not appear on a credit report. This includes debts such as utility bills and medical bills, ones that are expected to be paid in full and do not typically have payment plans, like credit card bills.

What Our Clients Say

No one likes to experience a debt problem. While there is no shame in getting help, the following testimonials redact the full names of actual clients of Heupel Law in order to preserve their privacy:

"We just want to say 'Thank You' for everything. Your people that helped us before the meeting were very professional and helpful. We are definitely recommending Heupel Law to others."
-C&D Valdez

"I would like to thank everyone at Heupel Law for helping us through this difficult time. Everyone we have dealt with is as cordial and professional as they could be. I am truly grateful for all of your help and should I ever encounter anyone in need of your services I will not think twice to refer them to you. You are all wonderful people and I cannot begin to express my gratitude for your help during the bankruptcy process."
-K&S Jackson

"After having financial difficulties for the past 2 years, I had no idea what to do next. I'd attempted filing bankruptcy on my own, and it was too overwhelming. I'd assumed that a lawyer was out of the question; way too expensive for my already exhausted budget. But, 2 months ago, I decided to research the option anyway, and that's how I got to where I am today. Heupel Law has provided all the assistance I've needed. I already feel like my life and finances are heading in a better direction."
-Alicia P.

"Heupel Law is one of the best, most professional law firms in Colorado. They offer flexible payment plans to help with your own finances and are the only law firm to care about our personal hardships in life as we were going thru this difficult process. From the first day we walked into their office, they have shown nothing more than kindness, professionalism, honesty, and care. They help you with anything you have questions about and definitely help guide you thru the entire process up until the end. Thank you Heupel Law."
        -A&D Medrano

"I want to thank Heupel Law. They made the filing for bankruptcy very informative about all the things that were going to proceed. They were very professional and very helpful in answering all of our concerns and questions. Thanks again for everything."
        -J&R Silva

"I was apprehensive about filing bankruptcy; concerned about what attorneys would think of me or how I would be treated by them. My first appointment was wonderful. Heupel Law was so friendly; non-judgmental and totally put my mind at ease. Since then, everyone that has helped me from Heupel Law has been so kind to me, so helpful and understanding. I am so happy I chose such a professional, non-judgmental and helpful attorneys like those at Heupel Law."
        -Kerry S.

"Filing for bankruptcy is never an easy decision. But my choice of using Heupel Law was not only a great choice but the right choice. I was put at ease as soon as I walked in the door. Great staff, great experience during hard times."
        -Paul D.

"I had someone tell me about Heupel Law and I also saw it on TV after my friend had given me the information. I was truly down and out on my luck and I guess by the grace of God I got this information. I was in an auto accident over a year and ½ ago and had not got any compensation for being off work. I owe thousands of dollars. I kept telling all the creditors about my situation and asked if they could work with me until I got back to work, but that did not go over so well. I have medical bills up the wazoo and of course lots of other bills pilling up as well. I finally went to my first appointment with Heupel Law and they were so helpful and understanding it actually brought me to tears. I was so excited about the overall idea about getting out of debt that all I could do was just keep bawling as tears just kept flowing down my face."

-Sennie C.

"After having been laid off from my job during the recession, I found myself in the very unfortunate position of needing to consider bankruptcy. I wish I had consulted with Heupel Law much sooner than I actually did, as it would have saved me $95,000, which I withdrew from my 401k as a way to make ends meet and keep my 800+ credit score. All I can say is while having to file bankruptcy is a difficult decision, after I accepted it; it was like the weight of the world was finally off my shoulders."

-Candace T.

"Having to go through a bankruptcy was a hard decision to make for me! The lawyers and paralegals at Heupel Law have made me feel at ease about the whole process. I have had help every step of the way and I am now feeling better about myself as things are starting to look up."

-Angela G.

"I owe a huge thank you to Heupel Law. I walked in feeling scared and stressed, but everyone made me feel welcome and at ease. By the time, I left a huge weight was lifted off my shoulders. Heupel Law made me feel much better about my situation. I was relieved and saw a light at the end of the tunnel. I truly appreciate all you have done for me. Thank you for helping me move on to the next chapter Debt Free. God bless."

-Donna B.

"When I had my first appointment, I was so impressed with the friendly staff, willing to help. It was so obvious that I was in the right place. They made it so easy and calming given the enormous stress surrounding me. There were right on top of everything and answered the questions I had. Such a friendly caring staff! Thank you so much for freeing me of debt!"

-Charlene M.

"I wanted to send a thank you letter to you for your services that you provided me with the Chapter 7 Bankruptcy. It has been over a year since the discharge but as I reflect back on how things unfolded, I can't thank you enough. Not just for getting the bankruptcy done but essentially for talking me through what the best options were and why. One year later I still feel so much more relieved than trying to manage everything myself. Although I am sending you this letter a year after our bankruptcy discharge, I still wanted to send it so that you knew how I felt and how things been progressing for me. Overall, I am once again thankful for how the process went. Thank you."

-Joshua N.

Incredible FREE Gift Offer

If you are struggling with debt, then get help.

Call (720) 443-4030 to schedule a **FREE Consultation**, which is normally valued at $197!

You'll receive the following benefits:

- Meet with someone who cares about your financial situation and wants to help you;
- Get an action plan to get out of debt;
- Receive recommendations you can trust;
- A money-back guarantee;
- Affordable payment plans;
- Rebuild your credit with "The 7 Steps to a 720 Credit Score";
- The ability to sleep at night; and
- Peace of mind.

There's nothing to lose except another sleepless night.

Take the first step and Call (720) 443-4030 to schedule your FREE Consultation.

About the Author

Kevin Heupel is a nationally recognized attorney in the area of debt relief and has helped thousands of good people get out of debt. Kevin Heupel has been featured in USA Today's Legal Elite, CNBC, and the Brian Tracy Show. Kevin Heupel is a contributor on Money for Lunch Radio. In March 2013, Kevin Heupel became a best-selling author on Amazon with his chapter: "Get off the Financial Roller Coaster", which was featured in the book: More Better.

Kevin Heupel is the founder of Heupel Law, one of the largest debt relief law firms in Colorado. Prior to starting Heupel Law, Kevin Heupel served as an Assistant Attorney General for the State of Colorado and was a corporate accountant. Kevin Heupel is well versed in solving complex debt problems and serving his clients with integrity and trust.

Kevin Heupel helps people find the right debt solution whether it is credit counseling, debt settlement, loan modifications, offers in compromise, student loan help, and personal bankruptcy. What sets Heupel Law apart is that Kevin Heupel offers free consultations, money-back guarantees, affordable payment plans, and education about restoring credit.

To learn more about Kevin Heupel, the debt relief expert, visit www.GetDebtFreeWithMe.com.

www.ingramcontent.com/pod-product-compliance
Lightning Source LLC
Chambersburg PA
CBHW071915200326
41519CB00016B/4625